RUNNING A MESSAGE PARLOR

By the same author:
Operation New Zealand,
published in 1970 by W.H. Allen, London,
and Whitcomb and Tombs, Christchurch,
and as
Bum Ticker: A Hearty Traveler's Tale, 1976,
Multinational Media, Scotts Valley, California.

Running A Message Parlor

A Librarian's Medium-Rare Memoir About Censorship

Gordon McShean

DRAWINGS BY TERRY DOWN

A Multinational Media Book

Ramparts Press
Palo Alto, California 94303

Library of Congress Cataloging in Publication Data

McShean, Gordon.
    Running a message parlor.

    "A Multinational Media book."
    1. Libraries — United States — Censorship.
2. McShean, Gordon. I. Title.
Z711.4.M32   098´.12´0973   77-72737
ISBN 0-87867-068-8

Published by Ramparts Press, Palo Alto, California 94303

First printing
November, 1977

Library of Congress Catalog Card Number 77-72737
ISBN 0-87867-068-8

Printed in the United States of America

This book is dedicated to Sensu

ACKNOWLEDGMENTS

Special thanks are due to the Pacifica Foundation for allowing me to use the recording "What Shall They Read?" to reinforce my memories and notes of the censorship debate in Richmond, California. The recording is available (as a record or tape) from the Pacifica Tape Library, 5316 Venice Blvd., Los Angeles CA 90019. It contains more testimony than I was able to transcribe, and gives you the thrill of hearing my voice!

I also appreciate the permission of Skip Taube of the White Panther/Trans-Love Tribe of Ann Arbor, Michigan, for use of the poem MAXIM 27 by J. D. Whitney. The poem was published in the book *Hello,* edited by John Sinclair and made available by the Artists' Workshop Press of Detroit.

I am indebted to the *Roswell Daily Record* for the numerous pieces of writing — and letters to their editors — which I used in compiling the story of the censorship controversy in New Mexico. The library press, too — especially *Library Journal,* the *Newsletter on Intellectual Freedom* and *Wilson Library Bulletin* — was of great assistance. Leroy Charles Merritt, now deceased, editor of the *Newsletter on Intellectual Freedom* during the time of the New Mexico censorship episode, deserves special mention for the encouragement he gave me during difficult times.

My gratitude to the numerous other individuals who helped cannot be expressed adequately. A list of their names would be lengthy, and I'd inevitably miss some of the most important. Some can be found subscribing to letters which are quoted in the book (and many quotable letters are omitted), but the majority must go unnamed. They can be assured of my lasting appreciation of their support.

Gordon McShean

Contents

1

The Outhouse

The Orkney and Shetland isles off the north of Scotland enjoyed plenty of secrecy during wars that made them strategic in the North Atlantic. There is still an aura of mystery surrounding them, for they have been neglected by the tourist trade — despite the beauty of the warm summer months there — and those who do know of them speak quietly of their charm in the knowledge that strangers would not believe the truth. The families who inhabit the islands, and who have contributed to a large expatriate population living in various exotic places around the world (for the Scots-Scandinavian islanders are inveterate wanderers) are close knit and possessed of certain proprieties. One of those proprieties involves topics of conversation which may be considered improper. As a student of anthropology will testify, taboos in a closed society can be quite involved. When such limiting conventions are improperly understood they can smack of moralism and drive a young person to a feeling of alienation. Especially if young, one can feel victimized when not sharing in the various conspiracies of silence. It was the secret surrounding matters pertaining to the outhouse which drove me to one of my earliest struggles with censorship.

It happened just after the Second World War when I was quite young. Each summer my parents would take my two younger sisters and myself on the long journey from Glasgow to our great aunt's croft near the town of Stromness on "the mainland" (actually the largest island, named Pomona on the maps). We would travel first by train, then on either of the ships *St Rognvald* or *St Magnus*, two smelly old vessels which invariably made us seasick. It was a holiday meant to build us up after the privations of the war and the strictures of rationing.

We would arrive at the port of Kirkwall, on the other side of the island, usually in the early hours of the morning. We would stand at the rail sleepily watching the stevadores unload the crates and the livestock from the ship while waiting for the arrival of an uncle with a car to drive us to the other side of the island. We were always a little anxious to get our feet back on dry land, and we welcomed the thought of sleeping on a wide mattress in the farm loft after the narrow, hard bunks of the ship's steerage section.

When the relatives arrived to pick us up we listened in awe to their strange accents (while they laughed at ours). We strained to keep our eyes open as we drove past the island's waist-high "forest" of shrubs (trees don't prosper in such a climate), and then looked for the silent and secret sentinels of the island's stone-age past, the Standing Stones of Stenness. Soon we would see the Bay of Stromness and my great aunt's croft. It was the kind of journey a youngster would never forget.

The islands still bore many of the scars of war. Fortifications were evident everywhere. But they could not spoil the quiet beauty of the rocky, treeless islands with their majestic crags and ever-present blackfaced sheep. The croft's forty-odd acres faced the town of Stromness from an ideal position. Since the sun hardly ever set on these northerly islands in the summer months, the bay was always glittering regardless of the hour of our arrival. It is a panorama which will remain in my memory as long as I live — perhaps because there was a time I was forbidden to talk about it.

It seems strange to credit the rough, earthy islanders with niceties which verged on the repressive, for life was not "nice" in the terms of city folk. When we first went, there was no outhouse at all, and the water had to be carried half a mile to the farmhouse in buckets. When nature moved, one used the byre where the cows were kept. The fact that one soon learned to know each cow by name didn't help very much. If cows happened to be there at the time, one had to learn to ignore their curious, bulbous eyes and concentrate on matters at hand. One also had to develop a fine sense of balance.

In company, you could talk of the byre without limitation — if you wanted to — but such conversation usually had to do with the twelve or more Aberdeen-Angus cows and the odd calf or two which we helped look after. Some of us would help in bringing them in from the fields in the morning and evening for the hand milking and even the children would manage to squeeze a little milk from the more placid cows. We all took turns at cleaning out the byre and trundling the messy wheelbarrow to the dungheap. There was little pretense in our conversation about such things. The croft was always filled to capacity by relatives and distant relatives throughout the summer, and I remember the conversation of a young cousin who was trying to relearn Scottish terminology after a stay in England. My cousin was walking with an uncle when she happened to tread on a wayward dollop of cow's turd.

"My goodness," said the uncle, "ye've put yer foot in shite!"

"No," said my little cousin seriously (she was only about four years old at the time), "I didn't at all." Her consciousness of the proper word was undoubtedly heightened by the many other vocabulary adjustments she had had to make in order to be understood. "It's no' shite — it's *sharn*" [the Scot's word for dung].

Such conversation was relished by the family because it verged on being naughty, and because the innocence of a child made it blameless. But it was so closely related to the everyday life of the farm that it was almost normal. We learned of life from the necessities of the farm. We learned the facts of life from the farm animals. I distinctly remember the special journey we made to take a cow to a "bullin'," and the concern of everyone in the farm when a favorite cow proved distinctly reluctant. There was no secrecy.

Other parts of everyday existence included the surroundings of the farm. There was a slaughterhouse nearby which stank to high heaven on the warmer summer days; the bellowing of the doomed animals which were sometimes harbored there sounded on the edges of our consciousness. At the edge of my treasured panorama of the bay the ugly tank of the gasworks loomed. And when bathing became a necessity we would all troop down to the "wee burn" which ran below the farm and eventually into the bay; we would splash each other and shiver in the chilly water, wondering why the soap never would create a lather in the peaty water. I personally hated having to bathe then, although I was ordinarily such a good little cub scout that I was remarkable for my fastidiousness.

We lived close to the earth, and colloquial conversation reflected this closeness. It was all the more surprising then that I should run into trouble over my subsequent references to the outhouse.

The outhouse appeared one summer after my parents purchased the necessary chemical container and an uncle was prevailed upon to construct the frame. We all enjoyed it a great deal even though the frame was rather makeshift, having been constructed of old lumber which had been lying about the farmyard. The outhouse even had a hook with which one could secure the door, ensuring a modicum of privacy which the byre had lacked in more ways than one. My father put an ash tray in it and called it the library, for many users spent long periods of time there reading the torn up pieces of the *Weekly Scotsman* which were hung on a nail and string for use as toilet paper.

My trouble perhaps stemmed from the unaccustomed comfort of the new facility. I had my own reason for dallying there, being still possessed of the idealism and innocence of youth — the outhouse had been built on an outcropping of rock removed from the cluster of the other farm buildings, and *it had one of the best views of the bay in the whole area.* I would sit there and watch the movements in the distant town reflected in the rippling waters of the bay. There were gaps between the slats of the door, and the result was all the more pleasing because of the framing effect. It seems I was the only one to have noticed it.

One day, in casual conversation with my great aunt, the new facility was mentioned. My great aunt was one of these ageless persons who is taken for granted in rural communities but who might be recognized as a sage in a more complex society. She was a very good cook, and did many things on the farm which strong men would hesitate to attempt, despite her slight and timeworn frame. If she was a sage she did not lack pride, however. She mentioned her pleasure at having such a beautifully modern convenience. "It didna' tak' Jim long to put the frame owr it," she said with obvious satisfaction.

My mother, who was sitting with me enjoying freshly baked bannocks with homemade butter — which the old lady had just taken off the griddle on the peat stove — nodded and smiled. "Aye, and he made such a good job of it, too — it'll last a long time."

"If the winter storms dinna blaw it awa'!" said my great

aunt, who was forever losing unlikely buildings and equipment in the seasons between our visits.

"Ye'll probably use the byre then, anyway?" asked my mother.

"Aye, the coos keep it rare and warm."

It was then that I had to get into the conversation with my tuppence worth. "I really like the new shed," I said. "There are geese and turkeys running about outside it, and besides, if ye sit in there on a nice clear day ye get the best view in the whole place!"

There was a long period of uncomfortable silence, fortunately broken by the arrival of a noisy bunch of cousins of about my own age who had to have bannocks too, and I was spared the full realization of the offense I had given. It was only later, when I had become aware of the hurt glances of my great aunt, that I became concerned and embarrassed by what I had said.

"Ye quite hurt her feelings," my mother said later. "What an awful thing to say — how could ye?"

I really did not know what I should be ashamed about. Why should one not comment on the beautiful view from the outhouse? Was she ashamed that the door did have gaping slats — was that something no good outhouse should have? Maybe they thought I was being sarcastic about uncle Jim's workmanship? I had really intended no harm by the remark.

Anyway, like all censorious acts, the repression I felt only stimulated me to wish to tell more people about the beautiful view from the outhouse. But I refrained, perhaps being intimidated by the likelihood of an all-island blacklist for me and my conversations. And so today I am belatedly inflicting my tale upon the reader in the hope that he or she will receive a vicarious thrill from having been the recipient of a forbidden message from the secrecy-saturated Orkney islands — now you know where to go to see the most outstanding view in the whole place.

2

Librarianship?

What makes a young man want to become a librarian? It was many years before I decided what I wanted to be — and even now I'm not sure I was right. If it takes bookishness (and perhaps it does) I was going into the wrong field. But I thought it had more to do with knowledge, imagination, things happening and — most of all — people-ishness (for what are books and libraries for if not people?).

I have often wondered what motivated some others to work in libraries — Mao Tse-tung and Casanova, for instance. But I guess they eventually gave in to other interests anyway.

My early bookish influences include hoarding a German grammar book because I had been forced into learning French in school — to the exclusion of German — "as the Germans were so bad in the war." Was I contrary — or were the school counselors?

I had a brief infatuation — unknown to her — with a clerk at the public library.

And at an earlier time I'd had an insatiable appetite for books with red covers (I swore they were invariably better than books of any other color, and wondered who knew my tastes so well and went to so much trouble to have them color-coded).

A turning point arrived when I had my library card removed after a conference of teacher, librarian and parent "because he is reading too much (three or four books a day) and it will hurt his eyes." I soon got around that. I still have twenty-twenty vision.

As I grew older my interest in history and politics grew. I devoured all kinds of odd history books, scouring the used book stores. I went out of my way to visit historical sites. This happened despite the fact that I was failing in history because "school history" was so dead.

I tried to borrow *Mein Kampf* because I had grown up hearing how terrible Hitler was in keeping the truth from people — only to find that the public library had joined his following and was keeping *Mein Kampf* from me. I borrowed the memoirs of Ribbentrop instead and developed a great sympathy for that misunderstood man. Maybe — I can't help thinking — a reading of *Mein Kampf* at that time would have kept me from developing such misplaced sympathies.

Then there were the sexy books. The colorless, puritanical Scottish environment could not help but inspire a young man to ogle the grey, grainy pictures of unclad breasts in books on African travel and exploration. I remember some earlier sexual stirrings when viewing the unclad cherubic creatures in line drawings in that classic children's work *The Water Babies.*

Soon I would advance to the early post-war paperbacks (found beneath my father's pillow). I particularly remember *No Orchids for Miss Blandish.* That book dealt with the debauching of a young woman through the use of drugs which were administered involuntarily. I read it and reread it and thought it very sexy. I recently came upon it again and searched in vain for passages which I would now call provocative. The Sears catalog was unavailable to me in these days, but if it had been available I would undoubtedly have considered it a pornographic classic.

I started off by saying that I was not a bookish person. But books did open vistas for me which were otherwise not yet accessible. I can only be thankful that I was able to make the transition from books to living life itself instead of spending my time reading about life and being an "expert." So many librarians and scholars think that the measure of the person who has a good grasp of life is his ability to compile exhaustive lists of books. If it was inevitable that I would become a librarian I wasn't ready to know of it yet.

I was just fourteen years old when a librarian showed how far some of the profession was likely to go in resisting the use of the library as an agency for change. In 1950 several Scottish Nationalists removed the Stone of Destiny or Coronation Stone from the throne in Westminster Abbey. The stone had traditionally been a symbol of Scottish royal authority, and the nationalists believed that its "captive" state in the English throne was an affront to Scotland's self-esteem. After some weeks of police failure in investigating the matter a librarian in Glasgow remembered that certain individuals had borrowed books which might have been useful in effecting the successful removal of the stone. The matter was reported to the police.

Persons who had borrowed books containing floor plans of the abbey and drawings of the throne were soon under investigation. A number of people were subsequently arrested and convicted who might otherwise have lived as free political activists and satisfied library users. They were jailed for the "crime" of using library materials for something beyond the satisfaction of simple intellectual curiosity — and of course for their failure to recognize how treacherous a librarian might be.

I began to wonder where the reporting of librarians might stop. I was myself a member of the Nationalist Party of Scotland and I sympathized (as would any young Scot with an appreciation of history) with the actions of those arrested. Half of Scotland sympathized with what they had done. Was every second citizen likely to be reported on by his librarian?

I had borrowed books on railways and the building of bridges, on revolutionary tactics, commando training and civil defense procedures, and on communism, fascism, spiritualism, antisemitism and witchcraft. All of this was in addition to the mysteries, travel books and psychology texts which I borrowed, partly because I was interested and partly because these books were most likely to have some sexual references in them. A man had a duty to learn some way or other!

I asked myself what strange kinds of conclusions law enforcement officers might arrive at if faced with a librarian-generated list of my reading materials? I had no respect for librarians any more, but the idea of the library's potential — if released from the stranglehold of the reactionary bookman — may have started to grow in me then.

3

Naughty Poetry

I have written elsewhere of the years which passed between my boyhood and my first library jobs. Some of the funnier episodes had little to do with censorship, and in retrospect the other things — which led inexorably to being a librarian — don't seem funny.

Even my library school training, which should have been challenging and informative, is hardly notable for anything beyond boredom and the stultifying routines which an authoritarian administration considered to be "education." If I had been in American universities a few years later I would likely have been saved from some of the tedium of that experience by becoming a student activist and demanding constructive change. But that consciousness was not yet abroad. I satisfied my need for social commitment by becoming class president and taking the poor, neglected foreign students on excursions to the town night spots.

A couple of generations previously there had been another Scotsman who had come to live in America and become involved in libraries. His name was Andrew Carnegie. He had financed the building of libraries all over America (and all over the world). Little did he know that his generosity might eventually seem a disadvantage to those of us who had to work — so many years later — in the buildings he had financed.

My first library "to call my own" was an old Carnegie structure in the town of Roswell, New Mexico. I arrived there with my wife, June (who will play an important role in this book), in 1966. Although the institution was grossly under-financed and under-staffed (one city counselor having recently asked, "Why do you need money from us — isn't Mr. Carnegie paying for your maintenance?") I had some stirrings of pride. I was head of the library of the second largest city in the state. It did not matter that my office was a dark cubbyhole in a corner of the building. It did not seem to matter that the staff room was also the basement storage room, a place where the unfinished brick walls and the heating pipes competed for one's attention while snatching a coffee break.

It did not matter that the town had for many years been the Southwestern United States headquarters for the John Birch Society (their bookstore had until recently been located across the street from the library), and that it harbored the New Mexico Military Institute. It did not seem to be relevant that some years previously the library and the staff had been under great duress because of charges of "Unamericanism" — when staff members had needed to have escorts if they left the library after dark because of the threats of political extremists who wanted the library to establish a propaganda "patriotism" shelf. All of that was in the past. The finances, staff and building might be meager, but the sun was shining outside (it is one of the sunniest spots in the nation) and I had my idealism.

It may have been an illusion, but when I first started to explore the facilities and came upon a portrait of Carnegie — stuck against some pipes, upside down, in the basement

storage area — his bearded Scottish face seemed to be looking into my bearded Scottish face in a bemused manner. I
was surprised when I reached to wipe some of the age-en-
crusted blemishes from the surface of the portrait, for some
strange illusion, caused perhaps by the shadow of my hand,
made one eye appear to wink.

Whatever happened, I thought to myself as I wiped the
rest of the grime away, the town is going to enjoy the benefits
of Scottish whimsicality again. I winked back at the old man
and carried him up to grace my cubbyhole. If nothing else I
would feel more secure having another beard for company
in that close-cropped town.

Soon townspeople were beginning to recognize the small
improvements we were able to make in the library, to note
the additions to the collection, and to warm to the changes.
Requests for talks on library problems, needs and potentials
(and on some non-library matters) poured in, and we began
to be very busy — almost too busy.

In the first few months we were also busy setting up
house, making friends, and exploring the area. We found
the people very friendly (we were to learn later that even the
people who disliked us were "friendly" — it is an old Southwestern custom, doubtless dating back to the days when you
could get your head blown off for not appearing friendly).

We made special friends of the symphony conductor,
an announcer on the local television station, the museum
curator, the owner of the town's only bookstore, the superintendent of schools, some of the directors of the community
little theatre, and the ex-librarian (who had happily become
a housewife after a romance with a well-situated rancher).
Listed like that our friends seem to have been an elitist clique,
but they were no such thing. All of these people were reaching
out into the community in some way. The town itself was
comprised of a number of closed societies. Newcomers —

especially if they had intellectual pretensions — had to hang together.

I won't go into the details of who belonged to "society" in Roswell other than to say that they had been there a long time and they affected to like "culture." They patronized the "intellectuals" now and again. They did not like Spanish-Americans. For those who were not part of "society" the nice thing about the members of society was their studied anonymity — it made their existence easier to forget.

My best new friend — from the viewpoint of a bookman, if not as a drinking buddy or the like — was Walter J. Geise, the proprietor of the bookstore. There were other places in town that called themselves bookstores, but they spent a major part of their effort in selling other things — gifts, souvenirs of the Southwest, religious articles, and even stationery. Walter's place was the only real bookstore.

I discovered his "Book Mine" a few weeks after my arrival in town, and had a great deal of fun browsing on the ceiling-high shelves of his little shop. We discovered that in addition to the book interests we held in common we were both passionately dedicated to freedom of expression. We abhored the activities of the censors. This was a happy discovery. It was also to have a great deal to do with what was to happen to us both during the next year.

Walter's shop contained some of the best books one could find anywhere. It also contained a rack of "adults only" paperbacks and a bundle of nudist magazines. He did stock some of the better classical erotica too. I rather enjoy that kind of literature, but he was inclined to apologize for all the "raunchy" stuff he had to carry (at least to me, who understood). He would rather have had a bookshop which reflected his own tastes — something no library or bookstore owner can afford to do.

"I would go out of business if I had to rely on the

people who come in here to buy good books," he said to me on one occasion. "There are so few who know a good book when they see one. But I still want to stock the better stuff if I can. So I subsidize the operation by carrying this other stuff. And I'm doing a public service" — he laughed — "some of these old boys come off the ranch once every two or three months, sell some of their livestock, then come in here to buy $50 worth of 'girlie' reading. It is a little pitiful, but I think they should be able to do that."

That conviction of his — that a person, particularly an adult, should have the right to choose his own reading materials — was soon to be challenged.

Soon our involvement in the projects of our new friends — the symphony performances, the little theatre productions, the museum exhibits (we did what we could as volunteers) — made us feel very much a part of the community. The success of the library-related programs we put on also fostered that sense. It was to come as a shock later to find that a significant part of the community did not feel that way about us. Perhaps the indications were there for us to see, but we were too busy and happy with what we were doing to notice.

Christmas in Roswell was a happier experience than we had anticipated. It was our first Christmas away from our families since we had been married. The library was gaily decorated, and so was our home. We drove to one of the forest reserves near the peak we could see from our patio, Capitan, and played in the snow. We paid a ranger for the privilege of cutting our own Christmas tree, and we had fun.

Our tree filled a whole corner of our living room, with the topmost branch bending a little where it touched the ceiling. It seemed we would never have enough decorations to put on it, but it was so pretty it hardly needed decorations. Underneath we spread the parcels we had received from friends and relatives in Scotland, California and other places, and then we sat by the fire. The fireplace completed our scene and made us comfortable at most times, but it was especially pleasant at Christmas.

We had expected the weather in New Mexico to be cold in the wintertime, but had found that although the temperature sometimes went below zero in the middle of the night, during the day it was usually quite bearable. I had a little more cause to complain about the climate than my wife, for I had occasionally to sit in my office without heat (or stamp around the building wearing an overcoat), since the furnace failed with annoying frequency.

Those of us in the library had little chance to feel sorry for ourselves, however. There were other "underprivileged" people in town whom we could serve with library materials if not with the other material needs they felt. The young people and the Spanish-speaking people were the most neglected in terms of the services we offered (like most libraries, we had always based our services on not the neediest but the most vocal: the middle-class, middle-aged, middle American). I instructed the staff on the new efforts we would have to make in order to balance the library's efforts. We would buy Spanish materials and hang signs in Spanish as well as English. We would buy more popular books and recordings for young people. We would not attempt to downgrade the collection for the people who already used it — we would just try to change the image of the library so that anyone might feel comfortable and satisfied using it.

I had started a program of news releases to emphasize our new direction. One of the stories ran like this:

LIBRARY RECEIVES BEATLE RECORDS

The librarian at Roswell Public Library is a Beatles fan. "Six weeks ago we bought records of the Beethoven,

Prokofiev and Dvorak pieces which were to be played by our symphony orchestra, and now we are acquiring records for the 'forgotten' younger segment of the town's population," said Gordon McShean, head librarian. The library has acquired four of the latest recordings by the Beatles.

Confessing that he personally owns a number of books and records by Beatles, McShean said he thought they were one of the most important groups of composers of popular music in recent years. He stated that he gave them most of the credit for taking the "yell and scream" out of rock and roll. "They are one of the few popular groups who have studied music seriously," he said. "It is not the long hair that counts, but what is under it."

The story went on to announce that the library had also acquired recordings of Welles's version of *War of the Worlds*, the documentary recording of the prelude to war, *Hitler's Inferno*, and "how to" records on the principle of flight, teaching children the facts of life, and yoga. It stated that suggestions for future acquisitions would be welcomed.

It was a new approach to public relations — at least for a public library in that area of the country — and the response was immediate and favorable. If any did feel resentment they stored it away for later use.

The personal treatment we had given the article reflected my philosophy that the town was small enough to permit such personal contact (approximately fifty thousand people), and my more specific feeling that the institution which has grown so big that it cannot relate on human terms is too big. It seemed to work. Library circulation of books jumped even though library use was falling off in other parts of the country and state. The fact that the town was losing part of its population through the closing of an air force base was not reflected in our figures.

My next library project grew out of a hobby of mine. It gave me cause, for the first time, to think in terms of the community's sensitivity to materials which might be considered controversial. I have frequently read poetry in public, and someone suggested that I could publicize the library's collection by reading the works of various poets in a series of programs. The anniversary of Robert Burns's birthday was coming up, and since he was one of my favorite poets (I read the dialect) I was hooked. I only paused to wonder if some of his poetry (especially the naughty verses which I prefer to read) would cause trouble.

When the evening of the first reading arrived there was concern that we might not have an audience. We had borrowed the museum auditorium in case we got a larger crowd than the library could hold. We were soon pleased with our foresight. By the time we were scheduled to begin every seat in the one hundred fifty-seat auditorium was filled, and ten minutes later there were people seated down both aisles and a group standing in the back.

The turn-out was most gratifying. It demanded every resource of talent in my repertoire. I had to shake off the librarian frame of mind and become a showman. I was a little nervous (later in the series I would be sensible and schedule other readers to assist me). Luckily my previous experience and the time I had spent preparing for the program at home paid off. The audience responded, even though it was obvious there were dialect words and phrases they did not understand. After a few nervous and tense moments at the beginning of the program everything went well.

> "When chapman billies leave the street
> And drouthy neibors neibors meet . . . ," I intoned.

With Burns' poetry explanations are almost a necessity,

at least for non-Scottish audiences. At this reading I soon found myself describing some of the intimate details of the poet's life which were reflected in sentiments expressed in the poems. The audience loved it.

I always attempt to relate to the materials I read, and sometimes I find an opportunity to interject my own sometimes humorous interpretations. Cold, lecture-hall type presentations are not for me.

As I stood and read the immortal lines from *Tam O' Shanter*

> They reeled, they set, they cross'd, they cleekit
> Till ilka carlin swat and reekit,
> And coost her duddies to the wark,
> And linket at it in her sark!

there were a few giggles from the audience. I was not sure that even a general understanding of the poet's meaning had been grasped. I felt it necessary to explain that the lines were describing the removal of clothes. There were glittering eyes and smiles all over the audience. I could almost believe that they had understood every word of the poem and that they wouldn't be shocked by anything.

As the program went on I became more and more bold and more and more pleased with my audience. I made references to poems in my copy of *The Merry Muses*, telling of the bawdiness which Burns had included. The audience was responsive to it all. I concluded that my estimate of their potential for narrow-mindedness had been in error.

At the end of the reading I was surrounded by admiring fans. I had two invitations to give readings elsewhere (one in another town), and many expressions of appreciation. A couple of kids wanted my autograph on the program.

By now it was clear that the series of readings was established — there was no turning back. As we left the hall I was almost ready to concede that I had made the proper choice of a career — but such thoughts are only momentary flashes, and in this case my success was hardly due to services which might be typical of library programs in general. The poets who would be featured in the programs in the future would be less controversial, less likely to offend, I thought. There was no longer any need to worry.

I turned to my wife as we walked to the car and asked her what she thought of the program. "Oh, I've heard you read better!" she said. I guess I should have known better than to ask.

4

The Little Minister

I was soon to find out that I had been lulled by a false sense of complacency. One lunchtime when I was sitting in the staff room with a couple of staff members, all of us eating sack lunches, two library clerks rushed down the stairs and asked to talk to me. The youngest girl was almost distraught.

"This man came up to the desk — he had these books in his hand — oh, I don't know how to tell you!" the girl said.

"He didn't have his dog collar on — she didn't know —" the older one said helpfully.

The younger one had regained some of her composure. "He pushed this magazine in front of me," she said, "and it was full of pictures of women with no clothes on." The girl trembled and stopped, obviously embarrassed and waiting for a sign from me.

She was a young lady I had hired from another town — there were few people in town with library skills whom I could call on; I could see now that she was too young to have been taken away from home. It was hard for me to give her the reassurance she needed. But she was gaining strength from the presence of the other staff members in the room. "Go on," I said.

"Well — if the other girls hadn't been at the desk I don't know what I would have done. He brought the magazines out of a paper bag, and I thought they were library materials he was returning . . . "

The other girl joined in. "When I heard her scream like that I really thought there was something wrong. Then I heard him yelling, and saw who it was. I came up to the desk as quick as I could so that she would know it was all right."

"I was really scared — not by the magazines, but by him," the first girl said, nodding. "Then he started yelling that this was the kind of stuff the library would soon have available for the children. He said he would be back to see the librarian, then he marched out."

"I think he was a little startled by her scream" the older one said.

"I really got a scare. Then she told me he was a minister."

One of the women eating lunch chipped in. "He is one of the ones backing the so-called anti-smut bill in the legislature now. He gets this way every now and again, particularly when he manages to get some laws drafted. Some day he'll have his very own book-burning. You'll get used to it." She went back to her coffee and sandwich.

"Thanks for reporting to me," I said to the clerks. "Don't worry about it, but let me know if anything else happens." Then I pondered aloud, "I wonder why he didn't come down to see me right away, if he was really concerned about the materials the library buys?"

"He did what he wanted to do," said someone sagely.

Someone else said jokingly, "Maybe he was afraid that if he showed you these magazines he'd give you ideas for some new additions to the library." We all laughed.

After the staff had gone back to their tasks I gave the matter more serious thought. The minister's action had very serious implications — and they had little to do with what we might buy for the library. For some months we had been working with the police department to attempt to catch a male exhibitionist who lurked in the library stacks. Twice we'd had the place staked out, but had caught no one. The women knew about the problem, but we'd taken pains to keep the public from finding out. The minister might easily have been mistaken for the sex prowler we sought. But aside from such considerations — which he was unlikely to have known about — it could easily have been asked why he chose to carry out his crusading in such an objectionable manner. What were his personal motivations?

There were larger implications for the library. The minister's misguided attack on us showed some interest by the censorship people in what we were doing.

I had heard that they were out to "get" my friend at the bookstore, but I didn't know of their plans beyond the attempt to have restrictive laws passed by the legislature.

Some sort of defensive action seemed to be called for. I checked with Walter to see if anything had happened at his store and was relieved to find that all was quiet there. When I went home that evening I wrote a letter to the editor of the newspaper. It was based upon an incident which had happened some weeks earlier.

The Editor
Roswell Daily Record

Dear Sir:

Not long after I became head librarian of Roswell Public Library an irate gentleman was steered to my office spluttering about the library having made a "dirty book" available to his sixteen-year-old daughter. I think the book he objected to was *Grapes of Wrath* by Steinbeck. At any rate, I welcomed him to my office, as it seemed his problem was related to one I was struggling with. I thought his opinion might be valuable.

At that time I was seriously considering combining the Young People's Collection with the Adult Collection in the main stacks because of shortages of both staff and space.

When I asked him about his ideas on the problem — before considering the one he posed — he was a little surprised. But he was soon rattling off reasons why there should be a separate Young People's Collection. I agreed with most of what he said. He said that if young people could find books suitable for them in one part of the library that would suit him fine; he wouldn't have to stumble over too many kids in the stacks when he was looking for books.

"Also," I suggested, "they might be less inclined to pick up books you might want to read, but that you wouldn't want your daughter to read?" He picked up the book from his lap, which was from the main stacks, and sheepishly agreed with me.

"I'll tell her to get her books in the young people's section until she is a little older," he said.

We still have the Young People's Collection in the library, and we will have for a long time to come, even though we have no funds with which to hire a Young People's Librarian and no space for new books.

I'm sure we would all be horrified if our reading material had to be chosen from a collection of books which was judged by booksellers and librarians as fit to be read by a sensitive twelve-year-old. Our old reliance on parents, teachers, and librarians to guide our reading habits has worked in the past; can any free nation condone blanket censorship or book burning in the name of morality?

But the new "anti-smut" bill [I cited the number] will do just that — make us lock up or destroy any book which might be deemed "obscene" with regard to the juvenile reader. And dad's old paperbacks with the girlie covers had better be put on a high shelf or he might find himself in trouble with the law for making objectionable materials "available."

If this bill goes through we will have lots of "Young People's Librarians" in Roswell. All your librarians will be buying young people's books and we might as well hang the "Young People's Collection" sign in front of the main stacks. Ironically enough, though, a prohibition on "sexy" books will do little to abate traffic in them — indeed it will probably stimulate their circulation, as the forbidden is always sought after.

I am of the opinion that responsibility for what a child reads should be primarily a parent's responsibility, with the teacher, the librarian, and perhaps the clergyman in the background to assist. Should we permit government control and regulation of this most intimate part of our lives?

I closed the letter with some information on the library Freedom to Read Statement, the general opposition of all librarians to censorship, and an appeal to concerned citizens to help us defeat the restrictive measures proposed in the state legislature.

I was placing a great deal of reliance on the effect a letter in the newspaper would have — and gambling that the letter wouldn't have a negative effect on what we were trying to do at the library. There was only one newspaper in town and it could be relied upon to carry our story, even if it occasionally carried something which worked against our efforts. Every few days it carried some political opinion or social commentary which made me angry, but I had to credit its editors with being down to earth and honest to their own viewpoint. There was one principal reason for choosing the newspaper: almost everyone read it.

This time I appeared to have gambled right. Shortly after the letter appeared the following editorial was printed on February 17, 1967 in the *Roswell Daily Record:*

NO MORE CHEESECAKE?

Newspapers in New Mexico might have to do away with cheesecake if the bill introduced by Chaves County Senators, S.H. Cavin and W.C. Schauer, passes the legislature and is signed by the governor.

The bill makes "dissemination of obscene materials to a juvenile" a felony.

To one mind, a picture of a starlet in a scanty attire might be obscene; to another, a picture of a nude in *Playboy* would not be offensive and would not appeal to prurient interests, which is one test of obscenity.

The point we make is that who is to judge what is offensive and what is not? The history of censorship is that what starts off as a good thing winds up with book burnings and a radical swing to Puritanism in its least desirable form.

Parents, still, remain the best censors of what their children look at and read.

Would a board of censors be established, or how would such restriction of certain books, magazines, etc., work?

We can think of some people who would make excellent censors; others we know, would veto anything — including Van Goghs. It appears to us that finding a board or public body without extremes of feeling on what is obscene and what is not would be nigh an impossibility.

Shortly thereafter the bill was killed in committee and the Roswell smut-killers were sent back home with the advice that they should get their community to draw up its own ordinances and not try to impose their views on the state.

The struggle had given us all a lot to think about. I could imagine the censorship people expecting me to attempt to deprave the minds of the town's youth by commandeering a bus on its way to Sunday School and taking all the kids to the library where I would insist that each would take a book while I chanted four-letter words in their little ears.

The fact was, however, that there was hardly anything in the town capable of arousing the prurient interest of a Spanish Fly addict on a fling, let alone a juvenile. Even the censors knew that. Even what was in the bookstore and on the drugstore racks was relatively tame. But the censors were determined to find something. The question remained to be answered: would they search for it in the bookstore or in the library?

5

A Seduction

Was I likely to use the library to corrupt? This reminiscence from my past may illuminate my motivations:

The tenement windows of the Glasgow suburb of Govanhill were like rows and rows of eyes, all concentrating upon the small patches of bare earth which were called — ironically enough — "back greens." In the corner of each back green stood a small doorless shelter filled with bins for the deposit of garbage and fireplace refuse. This was called the midden. Unless washing hung on the lines of any of the back greens (a circumstance which varied with the weather) children playing in these areas had the potential of a remarkably large audience. One or two small human outlines against such a grey, inhospitable pattern provided an attraction for the eye of the tenement dweller which could hardly be resisted.

Although I had two sisters, I tended to be a solitary child. I was always willing to please, and was known to be a good child not given to naughtiness. But there may have been some latent sexuality in the fact that I preferred pleasing females. It is a tendency I have never been able to overcome, whatever its motivation, and despite the pitfalls which were to befall me.

I was, as usual, cooperative when a certain Miss D. (who usually played with children who lived at the other end of the row of tenements) wended her solitary way to our back green and suggested a game.

"Chase me and see if ye can pull ma jumper off," she suggested, indicating her knitted pullover. Soon we were running from back green to back green, midden to midden, giggling. She wasn't a pretty child. She was about a year younger than I, and we both had a few years to grow before we would reach puberty. Her clothes were a little worn, and her toilette might have been performed with more care. But she was a bright child, and her features would mark her as handsome as she matured. But I was blind to all of that as I obligingly chased her about.

I suddenly put an extra effort into the game, and as I got close to her I lunged and succeeded in grasping her by the shoulders. I almost had enough of a grip to manipulate the pullover when she said "No, stop — ye'll mess up ma hair!" Like a good cub scout I stopped and waited for her to decide the next game. I would most likely have preferred being left on my own to dig roads and caves for my little toy cars, but I was nothing if not considerate.

"Ah'll tell ye what," she said with a gleam in her eye, " — see if ye can get ma knickers down. Ye won't mess up ma hair that way." With that she ran off and left me standing there wondering what to do. "Tee, hee, hee — can't catch me," she yelled. It was broad daylight and we were under all these windows, so I rationalized — although I knew there was *something* wrong with trying to take off a little girl's panties — that everyone would see that everything was honest, open and above board, so there would be nothing to worry about. I was still a little undecided when she stopped nearby, stuck her little bum in the air and flipped her dress so that I could see the object of clothing I was supposed to remove, then turned around and stuck her tongue out at me. Cowardy, cowardy custard . . . " she called.

How could a boy worth his salt ignore such a challenge? Soon we were running from yard to yard, giggling and laughing, with me grabbing at her legs and groping under her dress at the elusive knickers. Strangely enough I never gave a thought to the fact that if I succeeded in removing the piece of underclothing her bottom and her sex would be uncovered, nor did I have any sneaking thoughts of grabbing at forbidden territory while trying to win the prize of the game. I was young, and anyway that kind of thing never really came up. Such things were hardly ever talked about in the tenements, at least in the presence of children. I had merely wondered about such acts when they were mentioned in the half-understood formula jokes which were so often repeated and labeled "dirty." I knew the jokes were good for a laugh. I was in for a rude awakening.

I ran valiantly and soon had one hand snagged on the elastic of the leg of our chosen target, the other hand grasping her knee. She squirmed on the ground, squealing with delight, while I wondered if the material of her panties might give way if I pulled too hard, having a difficult time holding on to the tender young skin of her thigh with the other hand. I was just about to make a lunge for the top part of the piece of clothing — since she had raised both legs in the air to protest my "tickling" — when a voice froze us both in the middle of our movements.

"Stop that this minute!" The command came from one of the windows above, and the shock in the voice was obvious. We both turned to look for the owner of the voice and could see faces at a goodly number of windows, while curtains were being hurriedly pushed back in place at others.

We scrambled to our feet. Miss D. bit the knuckles of one fist while straightening her clothing with the other hand

(I had not succeeded in meeting her challenge at all, and there was not much rearranging to do). She looked at me conspiratorially then ran off silently. I didn't know whether to say goodbye to her or jump in the midden and hide. I felt a strange embarrassment about my hands — with all of these eyes on me the hands were guilty whether I let them hang by my sides or put them in my pockets.

"Come up at once!" I heard the unmistakable voice of my mother call. I knew I was really going to suffer.

"Ye were always such a good wee boy — what on earth made ye start to act like that?"

I was back in my own home, but somehow it was just as exposed to accusing stares as the back green had been. "Like what, Mum? We were just playing — "

"Don't try to fool me — everybody saw what ye were trying to do."

"But she suggested it — "

"Ye're a liar. Wee girls don't allow such things. Don't try to lie ye're way out of it."

"But I didn't even know what I was doing that was wrong — "

"That is enough! Your Dad will hear about this when he comes home!"

And so it came to pass. The adult male of the household used to emasculate the younger. And yet it must be said that the eyes of many of these tenement women reflected some kind of admiration for the innocent-looking boy who had a yen for the opposite sex at such an early age. The punishment at home relied on a spanking, but the greatest effect was gained from the subsequent not-talking-about-it; since sex hadn't been talked about before anyway the silence just grew deeper.

My confusion escalated when I was able surreptitiously to steal a look at some "answers to ladies' questions" in the conservative magazine *Woman's Companion* to which my mother subscribed. This led me to conclude that men are inclined to want to take liberties with women's underclothing, but that no decent woman permits this kind of thing unless there is a great bond of love, they are married to one another, the woman has ascertained the man's needs, and the woman has determined she is willing to suffer for the sake of her man.

I've concluded since then that if there is any communication which should be censored because of its potential for harm it is the communication which has already been censored, the teaching which tells only part of the truth.

Not knowing any better at that time, I had to admire Miss D.'s misplaced concern for me.

It took a frustrated and eager young member of the Girl Guides — some years later — to make me suspicious about the advice I had gleaned from the *Woman's Companion* and what had been said (and left unsaid) by my parents. Needless to say, I did not need the offer of a scouting proficiency badge to induce me to persevere in that effort, nature's own rewards being more than adequate. And by that time I had the good sense to attempt such good deeds concealed from tenement windows.

6

A Censorship Try

We settled down at the library to enjoy a period of comparative calm. I started planting trees around our home (trees need intensive cultivation on the high plains of New Mexico). We had twenty trees and I wanted twenty more. Our dog Shandy thought they were for him.

I gave a couple of poetry readings — Browning once, and a miscellany of children's verse another time.

Then one day a member of the John Birch Society "dropped in" to the library. He was in a good mood. He said that although he couldn't agree with my book selection policies he thought I was a good man, "basically."

"You can help us improve the reading materials in town," he said. "You wouldn't stand in the way of getting rid of the real trash from town?" he asked. "We have nothing against you or the library, you know," he assured me. "In fact, we think so highly of the library's operation that we'd like to help you get a decent budget."

I reflected that he was using the word "decent" in an indecent way. "Thanks," I said, deciding to be as pleasant as possible. I held myself back from asking about the strings attached to his offer. He left after some more polite conversation, neither of us learning much from the other.

Later someone told me there was to be a meeting to discuss the establishment of an organization to control the pornography on the drug store stands and in the book stores (they hadn't heard the library mentioned). I had heard that the drug store proprietors were ready to knuckle under any time pressure was brought to bear. They didn't want to compromise their other money-making interests. The Book Mine looked like being the prime target, therefore.

I went round to Walter's store as soon as I heard about the meeting. "They've told me they are going to close me down," he said. "Parents who don't know how to control their kids cause the trouble," he said with some bitterness, " — they'd rather drain a river than teach their kids to swim!"

I told him I would call every friend I could think of to attend the meeting. His rights and the principles of intellectual freedom had to be defended.

I called the other "big" librarian in the town — at the military institute — to see if I could enlist his support. He was also the editor of our local library association news sheet, and the holder of a number of posts in our state library association (I was to learn *which* posts later).

We had talked before, but never had explored professional principles. I had had doubts that one could operate a military-oriented library in a small town and still support free access to information as an everyday principle, but I was willing to be surprised.

"You-all know that I'm one hundred percent in favor of intellectual freedom," he said when I called, "But maybe they are right — in certain circumstances — when they call for us to keep trashy materials off the shelves." His voice sounded apologetic. "I have my doubts about defending *that* kind of trash!"

"Geez," I said. I didn't know what to say. I wasn't surprised — I was just unprepared. "We aren't defending trash, we are standing up for a principle — " I hadn't expected an outright confession of sympathy with the censors from him. "Geez," I said again. There was silence on the other end of the line so I started again. "They want to put Walter out of business — don't you understand that — the principle — "

"I'm sorry, Gordon," he interrupted.

"The principle," I continued, but hesitated because of the ideological chasm that separated us " — I never thought I'd have to explain basic principles like that to a librarian .... " I knew my attempt to communicate with him was lame and the implications of what I had just said were offensive. He didn't rise to the occasion.

I began thinking about all the information he must have been withholding from the poor kids at the school. There was still silence at the other end of the line. I started to boil over. "We need good book stores, good sources of information," I said. "It has never been discovered that knowing too much ever hurt anyone — it's what you don't know that hurts you .... "

"You don't have to explain nuthin' to me, Gordon," he said coldly. "Sorry, but I'm not going to be able to help you on this." *Click.*

I was furious, but by spending the rest of the day on the telephone I was able to bring together quite a number of people who would take our side at a meeting.

My expression — "It is what you don't know that hurts you" — turned out to be prophetic. Sometime later I discovered that this librarian was the New Mexico Library Association's regional chairman for the intellectual freedom committee. He held a list of names of people who were pledged to assist in just such a circumstance. His position would have assured us the support of the association. But by the time I learned this it only served to strengthen my cynicism about the expressed motives of my colleagues.

When we finally gathered for the meeting which could seal the fate of the bookstore the room was packed with friends and foes. We were in a large classroom at the YMCA, and there were more than sixty people packed into it. "It is almost as popular as a poetry reading," I quipped to my wife. She made a face.

The organizers started the meeting by showing us a film. It was blatant propaganda, blaming the international communist conspiracy, drugs and homosexuality for breaking down our sense of moral right. It combined moralisms and shots of some less-than-tasteful magazine illustrations to attempt to build up a feeling of offended dignity. It seemed to me so transparently biased that it was ineffective. But then I noticed the serious attention which was being given the film by a large part of the audience — at first I thought they were simply gaping at the "girlie" shots — and I realized that the makers of the film might have been right in their assessment of the intelligence of most of the people who would see it. Most were swallowing it hook, line and sinker.

As I looked around the room I could see the people who thought themselves morally upright — the ones who had come here to deprive a man of his livelihood because the knowledge he dispensed exposed their prejudices. I could see all these paragons nodding their heads in the darkness as pious cliches about the forces of evil were repeated one after another by the narrator.

When the light came on after the film the chairman announced that it would now be possible for us to speak in an objective and informed manner, now that we knew the dangers our American Way Of Life faced.

Nudist magazines were being passed among the audience.

The women were passing them on quickly with only a seemingly disinterested glance, but the men were taking more time with them, and every now and then a covert grin would appear on the face of an ostensibly disapproving male reader.

A young matron rose to tell everyone how she was afraid of what her son (twelve years old) might do after he had been exposed to the centerfold of *Playboy*.

I gasped. I thought I should leave before I got myself in trouble for telling them all how ridiculous they were. June counseled restraint, so I sat there. "I can't stand it, I know I can't stand it," I kept saying to myself.

I was relieved when Walter Geise got up and defended everyone's right to read what they want to read. He cited various historical precedents, quoted well known Americans, and went on at such great length that I'm sure a lot of people were lost. Walter is an earthy man who makes flowery speeches, and it must be conceded that it makes an interesting and not wholly unnatural combination. I enjoyed it.

Someone who knew that Walter ran the book store called out that he had a commercial interest in talking about intellectual freedom. It was an unfortunate truth. I wished that those without the commercial interest were as highly principled.

Walter's presentation was followed by a number of the drug store owners and managers who bowed contritely to whatever the will of the audience might be.

This got me hot under the collar again. I made a little speech. "How surprising it is," I said, "that knowledgeable businessmen will allow the conduct of their businesses to be dictated to them by a small pressure group — especially since the Chambers of Commerce boast of this being a land of free enterprise. There is no justification for calling for a restriction of trade when so many people in the community have shown that they approve of the material you are complaining of by buying it." I then went on to say that there had never been any proof offered that sexually explicit materials did any harm to anyone, young or old.

This started a stream of accusations about "outsiders" working to corrupt the town, and how it was all caused by the money urge — "pandering" was a word used quite frequently. The reference to outsiders was not lost on me, although I didn't see where anyone could say that I had a profit motive in keeping their media sources free from censorship. The word "pandering" was used quite unselfconsciously by an old lady who made much of the deterioration of morals which had occurred in her lifetime. I had to keep myself from pointing out that she had been in Roswell since the days when it provided all the "home comforts" for visiting cowboys.

Our supporters jumped to the defense, but wisely left the issue of outsiders alone — the prejudices in that argument were not amenable to reason. "Mr. McShean and Mr. Geise are both scholars, university men," one said, "and we should respect what they say." Walter and I cringed at this. The argument naturally had little effect on the opposition.

Another friend of our cause attempted to point out that the continuing concern with the money which was being made by those who sold the sexy books would be a lot less if the censors did not give the books so much publicity and make them so difficult to obtain. "That which is forbidden is always sought after," he said. But that too fell on deaf ears.

The leader of the censorship group asked for volunteers to be on three committees which would report back to all those who had placed their names in his register. "We only want to study the matter and see if action needs to be taken," he said, playing at being objective. "We are not condemning anyone at this stage."

Someone else suggested "Perhaps Mr. McShean would like to serve on one of the committees to see that his views are represented."

"I will not serve on any such committee," I said. "I feel that no group of individuals has a legitimate interest in enquiring into the rights of others to read what they will." My face must have shown my anger.

"Don't you believe in any discrimination in the choosing of reading materials?" a woman asked.

"Discrimination in reading is quite different from censorship of one's reading materials by others — if you don't know that I am sorry for you," I said, beginning to be provoked. All around I could see the blank, hostile faces of bigots. Our supporters had faded into the background of my vision because of the strength of feeling which had built up between me and the members of the censorship group. "You can't learn to discriminate if you have not read good books and bad books. How can children learn what a good magazine is if you restrict them to the *Reader's Digest?*"

June was pulling at my sleeve now. I should have known enough to sit down, but I was getting madder by the minute. "As far as I am concerned," I said loudly so that no one would miss it, "it is nobody's business what I read, what I think, or what I do in the privacy of my home, as long as I am harming no one else. I think that any reading anyone wants to do — or for that matter, any actions consenting adults may do between themselves — should be free from anyone's interference. I don't want to tell you what to read or do. You people should do the same and keep your noses out of everyone else's business!"

I was walking out as I yelled the last words. There was some scattered handclapping, but it only served to accentuate the silence of the rest of the group. June trailed behind me.

"I blew it, didn't I?" I asked her. I knew that talking about reading and proposing sexual freedom were two different things. I really felt shaken by what I'd done.

"They had it coming." June said.

"Christ, I wonder what this will do for my job?"

It was a dark, balmy night as we stumbled across the parking lot. We could hear the mumble of voices behind us as the other people at the meeting started to disperse.

"Don't worry about it," June said. "You can plant some more trees tomorrow and posterity will think kindly of you."

I gave her hand a squeeze. "Let's go for a drink." We both laughed and ran the last few steps to the car.

7

Strange Bedfellows

The John Birch Society man was back. He appeared to be uncomfortable as he sat in the old, hard library chair we had managed to squeeze into my cubbyhole office. He wore a very proper dark suit and tie. "I have an unusual request to make," he said, and paused as if for effect. I waited. He cleared his throat. "I want you to remove the John Birch Society books from the library shelves."

I couldn't believe that I had heard him correctly and my face showed it.

He continued. "We are afraid that some people who don't agree with our ideas will steal the books. Most of them can't be replaced. We want you to take them off the shelves and put them in a safe place." I must have looked incredulous. "If you can't do that, we'd like to have them so that we can monitor the persons who read them."

"I'm sorry," I said, "these are *our* materials — they belong to the library and the people of the city and county. Some were bought by us, and some were given to the town as a gift. They were put into the library so that people would be able to inform themselves about political beliefs. If I took them out I would be doing the public a disservice."

"But what if they get stolen?"

"If I base the materials in the collection on fear or intimidation — and I must say that the likelihood of politically motivated theft seems unrealistic to me — then I would be acting irresponsibly, wouldn't I?"

I gave him a crooked smile. "We may not always agree, but we have to know what we don't agree on. Controversial ideas must be available, or people will be unable to evaluate controversy. My first responsibility is to make the materials available. I would have an additional responsibility to see that stolen books were replaced and thieves prosecuted."

He was looking down at the floor now. "Then you won't take them off the shelves, even at our request?"

I had a feeling I was being tested. I looked at the man and his pressed pants and shiny shoes. I felt sorry for him because he lived in fear of so many bogeymen (perhaps I was one of the hobgoblins who inspired his fear). "I'm sorry. No."

There had been no mention of any other works of controversy, although the recent meeting to rid the town of sexy books was obviously in our minds. Walter's store was still open, and we both knew it. He started to leave and I rose to show him out.

"How are things at the library?" he asked.

"Just fine," I said, smiling. I could see the feeling of relief on his face as we approached the library hallway — but I gave him credit for the fact that he may simply have been relieved to get up out of our hard chair.

I was glad it was Friday and we had the weekend to look forward to. I had deliberately not scheduled any library activities, for once.

That weekend June and I drove to Ruidoso, in the mountains some seventy miles away. The trip seemed longer, but it was worth it. The road began to twist and turn as we gained elevation, and trees became more numerous. We were soon passing "Indian Museums" and Mexican fruit stands — but the tourist season hadn't started yet, and most were deserted. The orchards looked pretty, but I looked forward to the evergreens we would see higher up.

We passed the awful, regimented line of buildings which housed the Ruidoso race track — made especially ugly because it lacked horses at this time of the year — and soon were in the quaint resort town full of cabins and evergreen trees. As we traveled we had caught glimpses of the Sierra Blanca winter resort area as the road climbed, but we had no interest in visiting there. We had developed the habit of stopping at a little rustic restaurant where we would eat Indian corn bread sandwiches. This weekend we were in for a special treat, for "Chief" sat with us at the hearth in the restaurant's lounge area and told us about his Indian background. He was the proprietor, and he had previously made us feel at home by talking to us about the Roswell happenings he read about in the newspaper. This weekend he and his wife devoted themselves to us — we were the only people in the place, with the exception of a large and garrulous Texas family who needed no company but their own after they had been served.

This weekend the chief's wife sat down at a small organ which we hadn't noticed before ("I'm usually too busy to play" she said, half apologetically) and entertained us with a selection of old favorites while she carried on a conversation — it was a display of unselfconscious virtuosity that amazed and delighted us. We emerged into the brisk mountain air quite rejuvenated, and wandered about the town on foot, letting the dog run. It was an outing we would long remember.

When it was time to return to Roswell we detoured through the old Western towns of Capitan and Lincoln. They still survived on the notoriety of the range wars and the fame of Billy the Kid shooting McSween. But soon the land became less majestic, lying flat before us, and the road into Roswell ran straight and easy. The problems of the library were back in our minds. We wondered what Chief would be reading in his newspaper about *that*. But we consoled ourselves with the knowledge that he only paid attention to the happy news.

It was a few days later that the John Birch Society man returned to the library. I happened to be at the service desk when he arrived, and I started to walk with him towards my office. As we passed the table marked "Sale of Discarded Books" he stopped me. There were a number of volumes for sale, most for ten cents, but some as high as a dollar.

"It is this I had come to see you about," he said.

"Fine," I said, pointing him into my office and the hard chair. "I take it I can't sell you a book?"

He gave me an angry look. "Did it every strike you that you are selling public property?"

"Sure," I said. "Government offices sell their surplus all the time. They would be irresponsible if they simply destroyed it. And it could lead to graft if they gave it away. Can you think of any better way to get rid of our discards and the gift books that we can't use?"

I could see that I wasn't pleasing him by being so glib, but the answers all seemed so obvious that I couldn't help myself.

He changed his tack. "What bothers me is that you take books out of the collection at all. These books were bought with public money. What right have you to get rid of them? They should stay here for ever!"

It was all I could do to keep from laughing as I answered that one. "Surely you know that knowledge advances — that better books become available — and that some books just become so worn that we can't keep them from falling a-part . . . ?"

I got up and motioned him outside to look at the books on the table. "My 'right' to dispose of them in a responsible manner is my *responsibility* — it is part of good library management."

He seemed reluctant to examine the books, as if afraid to find that my words were justified. "Look," I said, "here are old yearbooks, out of date. And we have a book on travel in India from the 1940s — the collection contains much better, up-to-date material on the subject. Here is an ugly old novel by someone we never hear about any more — it hasn't been checked out in years. Here are some old children's books that are just falling apart; they have been replaced with new copies."

He looked at a few of the books I had pointed to, picking up one or two to examine them.

I went on. "It would surprise you how many people will want to own these — and it would amaze you how much these dimes add to our budget in a year!"

He turned around with a gleam in his eye, and I could see that he thought he was about to claim a victory. "But you are in competition with free enterprise — you are taking the bread out of the bookseller's mouth!"

"You're kidding!" I said. "My friend Walter at the Book Mine is the only person in town who sells used books — and he buys an odd volume here, occasionally!"

The man's shoulder's slumped slightly. His eyes roamed over the collection of discards. They settled on a set of prettily bound coffee table novels which had been printed at the turn of the century. They had been found in someone's attic and donated to the library (I had spent some of my evening hours collecting these and others). I had listed the set for sixteen dollars. "What are these?" he asked.

"It is a nice set," I said. "But the library seldom uses sets because the authors don't file in the right place — " My apologies weren't needed, however. The man coveted the set. Within a few minutes, after looking about the other materials on the table, he had decided to give us the sixteen dollars.

As I was taking his money he asked, "By the way, how *is* your budget?"

I confessed that the prospects for sufficient funds to accomplish the programs we needed weren't bright, but said that we had started to organize a "Friends of the Library" group to try to get our message across.

"If I paid the dues, could I be a 'friend' too?"

I nodded.

Suddenly there was more money on my desk. I was momentarily pleased. Then I had time for reflection.

"Who needs enemies when you have 'friends' like that?" I asked myself.

8

Children Again

The summer months were as busy as any others for us. We had to implement some of the changes I had proposed in order to work within the limited budget. This included moving the entire children's collection from its basement location to the main floor (we had previously closed the children's collection in the early evening because we lacked the staff to keep two desks going at once).

It was nice to have an "integrated" service desk, with the children closer to the center of things. We had an ancient "grandmother" clock on the wall of the library, and a model of an "original" oil derrick which had been made by an old-timer sat close-by on the top of a bookshelf. The children were crazy about them.

Introducing strangers to a library is always difficult, since every-day users take its services for granted (and that includes librarians). The clock and the model helped us start a give-and-take with the children to allow us eventually to talk about more mundane subjects — like what new children's books we had in the library.

I had discovered quite early that you can't simply ask children what they want in the library. You have to talk to them about things like grandmother clocks, oil derricks and electric erasers (they loved that piece of equipment, being impressed by the fact that we made so many mistakes that we needed electric-powered assistance to wipe them away) — and then mention the other things in which we might have a mutual interest.

Sometimes a poem helped bridge the generation gap. I enjoyed having the opportunity to indoctrinate these young minds with my ideas of what a particular poet meant, and they appeared to enjoy it too.

Soon I found that I was not only in demand to show children around the library (climbing up to wind the clock — even if it had only been wound a few hours previously — running the electric eraser and making copies on our copying machine) but I was also being invited to visit classrooms in Roswell and towns nearby.

I found myself with audiences ranging from kindergarten to high school, and with poetry recitation requests ranging from Mother Goose to Chaucer in Old English. I still like to read the letters I received — I had huge bundles of them from the younger ones (teenagers hardly ever wrote).

Once, while visiting a group of very young children, I was asked about my beard (this was a close-shaven community, remember). I told them I had had it almost as long as I could remember (which was *almost* true), and added, "When I grow up I am going to be Santa Claus!" I can still see the wide eyes of the children who were the innocent recipients of this bit of intellectual irresponsibility.

I had another project which proved most popular. I introduced paperbacks into the collection — masses and masses of them, on drugstore racks which I had managed to obtain from the paperback supplier. Within a few weeks our circulation of hard-cover books had dropped 5 percent, but our total circulation had increased by 5 percent. Ten percent of our circulation was in paperbacks! Subsequently we did hear rumors about "influential" people who were unhappy about the paperbacks. There was even one report of an individual who was laying the groundwork to "get" me on the basis of the paperbacks we had, and he could be seen every now and then examining the materials which had the more lurid covers with a more than passing interest. But nothing ever came of that.

I had some vacation time due, and we were able to relax a little during a vacation-cum-conference trip in San Francisco. I enjoyed the chance to meet some of my professional friends as well as the opportunity to visit our families. Everyone wanted to know how we were doing in New Mexico.

While I was at the librarian's conference a very influential educator cornered me and said "There is a great opportunity for you to go back to school and earn your doctorate at government expense. Why don't you apply? I will do my best to see that you get into the program."

I was flattered that I should be given this attention. I took only a few seconds to consider, and then said that I was too busy with the library in Roswell. I had only been there a year, and I owed them more than that, I said. I felt very dedicated and noble. But there was nothing I would have liked better than to have gone back to school to gain the Ph.D.

One of the highlights of the trip was my visit to the Haight-Ashbury district. I "invaded" it with a number of other daring librarians, and we had a very good time. We talked to a great many freaky people. We gawked, bought posters, buttons and books of poetry, and generally behaved like tourists. The merchants and the street people made us feel welcome, but I felt about as out of place as a John Birch Society man in a library. It was too bad that that relaxed, "groovy" environment would be no more in another year or so. I can't help wondering if they sold more than their discards.

When we got back to Roswell the summer had peaked and the children were thinking of their return to school. Everything was green from the summer rains. The community theatre group was busy choosing plays for the winter season. It was a time ripe for change. We still contemplated our future cheerfully. We still had our innocence.

9

Going Psychedelic

It was lunch time, and I used the opportunity to enjoy the late summer sun by walking the few blocks to the office of the president of the library board of trustees. I wanted to talk over a few things informally, and now that I had been with the library a year members of the board didn't seem to mind if I would drop in on them.

I was received cordially. "Libraries always seem to drag just at the end of summer," I said. We discussed programs for the autumn. "We need a big program to get things started," I said. He nodded.

I went on. "I was wondering if I couldn't do something to liven things up a bit by having a poetry reading *in* the library. We've always had the readings in other halls because we lacked the space. A lot of people don't know what we suffer in that old building. Maybe we could gain support for a new building from some more people and get a few of them to borrow a book of poetry?"

The board president was getting ready to go on his vacation and I knew his mind wasn't really on the library. "How would you squeeze all of them into that little building?" he asked.

"I figured I could have them call in to make reservations," I said. "Then when I got more than thirty or so I could start taking names for a second reading. We should be able to jam that many people into the building. Anyway, I wanted it to be a little, intimate gathering — the other readings have been too big. If I ever read for a hundred seventy people at one time again, I hope it is for money!"

"You might be able to make some money if you are taking reservations," he said jokingly.

"It might not be a bad idea to solicit a donation for the Friends of the Library, huh?" I asked.

He nodded his head in enthusiastic agreement. "I'm sorry I'm going to miss it, Gordon," he said. "Do you have some good stuff to read?"

I brought out a bundle of poetry collections I had picked up on my visit to California and dumped them on his desk. "It is all contemporary stuff," I said. "We have hardly given the modern poets a chance in our previous readings. I've got this stuff, and some poetry from local enthusiasts. I might even read some of my own. I've no idea how contemporary poetry will go over here, but maybe it is time we tried something different."

He glanced through some of the materials. "It looks interesting to me," he said, "but I honestly don't know if anyone will come to listen to it."

"How would it be if we billed it as 'hippie' poetry, and lit some candles and incense — gave the library some atmosphere?"

"It sounds great, Gordon." He was looking at the poems again. "Do you know which of these you might read?"

I shook my head. "I'm not going to read anything real wild — you know me — I play to my audience. I thought I'd add my usual explanations of what the poems mean to me."

"Do you think we should maybe keep the kids out — make it an *adults* only program?"

I said that I didn't think anything I was likely to read would be likely to bother kids. "Adults get offended quickest," I said. "If you think it is advisable, I'll go along with a requirement of parental permission for kids who don't come with their parents. You know this town better than I do. But I don't go along with banning kids entirely."

He said that suited him fine. "Go to it, Gordon!" he said. "Lots of luck!"

"Have a good vacation!" I said.

I walked back to the library to start looking over the poetry more seriously. There was a lot of good material, most of it from small "art" newspapers that I had picked up in San Francisco, and I knew it would not be difficult material to present in an interesting manner. I was elated that we might now have a chance to draw attention to the inadequacies of the library building by scheduling the readings there.

We started the publicity immediately in order to try to gauge the interest of the people in the community and the demands which would be made on our facilities.

There was no requirement to clear the program with the board of trustees — any more than there would have been a requirement to check book purchases with them — since they had approved the series of poetry readings in principle at the beginning of the year.

Our library display case began to attract attention for the program immediately. I had taken the "artier" pages from the newspapers I had picked up on the coast and used them to brighten the library. There were pages from the *Berkeley Barb*, the *San Francisco Oracle* and the *Los Angeles Free Press*, the three most popular "underground" papers in the West.

The display leaned heavily towards American Indian imagery (as did some of the poems I planned to read). That was fine for a place like ours which had so many cultural and historical ties with the American Indian. There were also a few "pop" art pieces, and some quite traditional and ordinary line drawings of pastoral scenes.

But color was the most obvious thing about the display — the newspapers jumped out at you with their brilliant, contrasting illustrations and designs, native, traditional and pop. I had taken some day-glow poster paper and made a sign which read "PSYCHEDELIC" NEWSPAPERS FROM CALIFORNIA.

It was an eye opener for the people of the high plains of New Mexico. Many were unaware of the American Indian influence in the art work on display. They were too busy looking at the ordinary news photographs which appeared on the edges of some of the color pages. One showed a number of long-haired youths leaning with their hands against a wall while police searched them — a typical "bust." In another picture a young woman was being dragged along the pavement by a policeman — by her hair. A small news item also caused some interest. It was a report on what was happening in China. The article could be interpreted to be pro-Mao. From the interest shown in the display one might have thought that the stuff had been brought from a foreign country, it was so strange to those who viewed it.

Some of the comments were run-of-the-mill. "Pretty" and "interesting" were frequently heard and relayed to me by staff members. But there was one comment, overheard by mistake, which gave us cause to be concerned. Two elderly ladies had studied the materials for some time. "He calls it psychedelic," said one to the other, finally, "but we know what he *really* means, don't we?"

"Yes, indeed," the other replied, nodding sagely, her

words heavy with some hidden significance. "We know what he means."

I hastened to look up the word "psychedelic" when I heard the report of that exchange, but the dictionary didn't give me a clue to the deeper meaning the ladies had knowledge of. I puzzled for a long time over what someone else might think of the purpose of my choice of words and the subject matter. I had previously thought the exhibit might contribute to understanding. I had enjoyed putting it in. But now I had cause to question my own idealism.

During the week I had been offered a chance to apply for a library job in a much larger town at almost twice the salary I was making in Roswell. I had turned it down, citing the same feeling of "owing" the town something. Now I began to ask myself if I had a right to feel idealistic about what I was doing. A mediocre success with a display case, efforts marred by misunderstanding, and a low salary to boot, were hardly the components of a program to give one a feeling of doing something worthwhile.

I began to have even more doubts when I attended a meeting of the library board later in the week. The board members were at a loss because the board president was on vacation. There was some confusion and uncertainty when I mentioned the projected poetry reading which the president had okay'd.

"Can you show us some of the poetry?" somebody asked. I still hadn't made a firm decision on the poetry I would read so I passed around a bundle of the items most likely to be used. There was an antiwar poem by Gary Snyder that I was sure I was going to read and a few other things I could be positive about.

I gave them a general idea of the subjects I would try to cover. "I hope there won't be any objection to the antiwar material," I said, "because I couldn't really represent the feelings of the poets if I didn't include that." There was no reaction from any of the board members. "I'm also going to have to include something on the drug experience. It is just like the problem with reading Robert Burns — you can't read his poetry without mentioning women and booze."

An older lady board member was shuffling through my materials now. She came to a page which had a line drawing of a nude young woman, posed decorously. She pursed her lips, bundled the materials together, and threw them down on the table. "I find this quite disgusting," she said.

I felt like saying, "I'm not giving an art show!" but I held my peace. I felt that I should be able to give art shows too without being faced with the narrow moral judgments of influential community representatives — but that was another argument.

Another of the board members was inclined to be more reasonable. "I think it is all right for you to give this reading," he said. "After all, you did clear it with the president." There was no requirement that I clear any library materials through anybody — responsibility for presenting balanced programs lay with me. The president had only been brought into it because I had been uncertain about how the material might be viewed by the community, and as a courtesy. But this was no time to argue that either. I let the remark pass.

The board member went on, "I would like to know, however, if you couldn't maybe ban the kids from the reading entirely?"

I shook my head. "There aren't going to be any offended kids," I said. "I only agreed to limit the attendance to parental consent because I thought we might have trouble with *parents*."

The man still looked worried.

"It is going to be all right — honest!" I said. "I only do wild things when I've had a few drinks with my best friends." I smiled. The board seemed to be reassured, although the older lady still seemed determined to believe that I was promoting the work of the devil.

Now it was another board member's turn. "I think it is okay for you to put this program on," he said. "After all, your other readings have been very well received. But I want to know why you can't do it in another hall?" The other board members were suddenly nodding enthusiastically, and smiling at one another. "Why can't you do it in another building, like you did the other readings? That would keep us from risking any trouble about having something like this in the library."

I sat and shook my head again, looking at each in turn. "I'm sorry to appear so stubborn, but there's a principle involved. It is precisely for the reason that you just gave — that we should try to safeguard the library — that I am insisting that the program should be in our building. If we allow anything to be kept out of the library for fear of reaction — especially when we know it is something worthwhile — then we are laying the groundwork for other things to be kept out in the future. It is censorship."

There was a lot of paper shuffling and some throat clearing. I wasn't sure that I had gotten through to some of, them. "This board claims to endorse the Library Bill of Rights," I said, "and yet you would take an action that would only satisfy those who oppose these rights." I indulged in a little rhetoric. "We post a copy of the Library Bill of Rights — as does most every other library. It informs the public of the impartiality of the library's procedures. You have to be courageous to stand behind that. If we are going to be safe we shouldn't endorse things we don't believe in."

Everybody looked gloomy. There was silence for long moments. I finally broke it. "I *could* move the program out if we were being swamped with reservations to such an extent that the library facilities would be strained. I could go along with that. That would be an honest reason." I shuffled my papers and checked off a few subjects on my copy of the agenda for the meeting. "Who knows, we may get that many people wanting to hear it."

The glum looks on their faces slowly started to change, and within moments the company looked decidedly happy. I hadn't intended to offer a deal, but that was the way they were taking it. A sharp board member proposed a motion that the librarian be authorized to engage another hall for the library's next poetry reading if the number of reservations warranted it. It was a small victory for me, for it meant the board had approved the reading in principle. They went on to other business.

Afterwards some stopped to make reservations for themselves and friends. Although the reading had not yet been announced (it would be in that afternoon's paper), it was half subscribed after they and the staff had made their requests.

The meeting had been held in the early afternoon because we were still on a summer schedule. A few hours later, after the newspaper had appeared, I was still busy making telephone calls to try to find an alternative place to hold the reading. My staff members were on the other lines, taking incoming calls, confirming long lists of reservations with the proviso "if we get a hall."

There weren't very many places in town where one could hold a poetry reading, especially if an audience of any size was expected. Hours of telephoning (many places required me to keep calling back "to talk to someone with the authority to say yes or no") had done no good.

It seemed a very unusual circumstance that every hall and conference room in town would be busy on the same night — especially since so many people were asking for reservations and could be presumed to have no other out-standing commitments. It appeared that the word had spread around town like wildfire that I was planning to put on some very disreputable type of program, and there was hardly a hall proprietor who would risk being associated with it. Even my friends at the schools and the museums found a reason to make their apologies.

There was one hall owner who seemed most anxious to play host to the poetry reading: the proprietor of the town's teen club, who had already suffered a great deal at the hands of the "respectable" people in town. He went so far as to promise to provide a set, background music, and arrange for special lighting. He would even cooperate if we wanted to make a commercial venture out of it if the library dropped the sponsorship.

Some board members became aware of the offer and were decidedly unhappy. It seemed to confirm the opinion that the program was not suitable for "proper" people. A board member instructed me privately to schedule the reading in the library rather than accept such an association with our program.

But while there was still a chance that another site might be found board members continued to call me for news of progress. I began to lose patience with some of those who were so candidly anxious to have my program removed from the building — their attitude seemed hypocritical, to say the least. But they kept reminding me of my own statement about the need to move to a larger hall if reservations proved to be too heavy. By this time we could have filled the library a couple of times with the people who had made firm reserva-tions for the first program; we had a waiting list and were promising to contact people with information about subse-quent readings.

My telephone calling had reached a dead end. I had

tried every place which might have been suitable and had been turned down. I called some of the key board members. "Even the hotels, motels and inns have filled their larger suites," I said. "We may just have to have the program in the library after all."

This news resulted in some frantic activity by those who "Knew somebody who would help." But these contacts weren't going to work in this circumstance either.

When a board member finally called me with the news that their efforts had been useless and that I might as well plan to have the reading in the library he could tell I wasn't surprised. "I've been figuring how to arrange the chairs," I said.

"You are hopeless, Gordon," he said, laughing.

"It is going to be cosy."

Shortly afterwards I received word that the city council had met and had discussed the library's proposed poetry reading. This was reported to me by the husband of one of the staff members. The matter had been admitted as business although the report of their informant was based solely upon rumors. No library board member had been asked for information or told that library business was to be covered, although that would have been proper. The result was one that would cause us dismay and subsequently cause the aldermen some embarrassment.

A number of ill-advised statements about the library had been made. "There's a lot of weird things been going on down there," said one alderman. "We should fire that librarian," said another. After a lot of such enlightened comment a vote was passed cutting all funds from the library unless the program we had scheduled was canceled.

"Damn fools," one of the board members growled to me over the telephone later. "They should have known that they can't make an action like that stick. They didn't consult us and they didn't even ask the city attorney if they could do it. We have to be committed to our program after they do a stupid thing like that. All they've done is guarantee the city lots of unwelcome publicity."

His words proved prophetic. The wire services carried the news nationally. Reporters began to call the library, and some even traveled considerable distances to gain interviews. We did what we could to keep the coverage from misrepresenting the situation — the truth may not have been bad, but it did seem silly!

The furor that resulted had the unfortunate effect of confirming the members of the council in their mistake, at least until such time as they could meet again and put matters to rights — if they got the right information! Meantime, when questioned, they invariably found some pretense to justify the action they had taken.

We were consoled with the knowledge that the council did not really have the power to coerce us with threats of withdrawal of funds. They had already committed the money to us during budget hearings earlier in the year. But they could eventually harm us by taking such action on future budget requests. We were comforted by the thought that they were making themselves look foolish by doing all this over a program which was unknown to them.

I still had to make the program up, present it, and somehow justify the stand we had made. It was a small consolation.

10

Blasphemy

Another flashback to my youth appears appropriate here:
I really did try to be good. I was a cub scout with
masses of badges sewn on my blue pullover. I marched with
the scouts to the Scots Presbyterian Church once a month,
snapping my "eyes right" on command to salute all the dig-
nitaries who gathered after the service on the church steps.
I never carried a knife except for scouting. I never cursed or
swore.

And when I was out playing I was careful to be good.
Sometimes I took little deaf-and-dumb David with me and
showed him hideaways and good places to fish for tadpoles.
I marked trails for other people so that they wouldn't get
lost. And when there were no pennies for me to purchase a
ticket to see the serial version of *Superman* at the children's
cinema, I sometimes went to the Evangelist's Magic Lantern
Show in the ex-army hut to try to find God (*they* had pictures of Him which we had never seen — being forbidden
graven images — at the Presbyterian church of our scout
troop).

When I was at the evangelist's with the other children I
did my best to let Jesus come into my heart when they showed
that picture of the man with the beard knocking on that

little door. But somehow I knew I didn't have a little door in my heart.

When the evangelist and his wife (she playing the piano a little out of tune) had us sing, I sang loud and clear to let God hear me (for they assured me He was there). But lots of things about the evangelist's message perplexed me. We were nearly all from poor families living in rented cold-water flats, so when we sang "The Wise Man Builds His House Upon the Rock" I couldn't help wondering *who had a house?* — and *who among us would ever build one?* The evangelist said "In my Father's house there are many mansions," and I hoped they would be better than tenements and wondered what the weather would be like. I did like "There Is Sunshine In My Soul Today," and would sing that with all my might because I loved the sunshine and was reminded of the too-few bright days we enjoyed when we'd walk to the edge of the city and enjoy the green hillsides and the fresh air. It was heavenly to get away from Glasgow.

In that song, however, there was a line which said " . . . for Jesus is my Light," and that bothered me. Jesus was a bearded creature in a sheet who haunted Presbyterian Sunday School basements and ex-army evangelist's huts (shaded to make the magic lantern slides visible), hardly a creature of light, let alone sunshine. But I got bookmarks and colored stick-on mottoes for attending the evangelist's shows, and the assurance that God knew I had attended. All that remained was for my heart to let Jesus in and be filled with light so that His (and our) Father would write my name in His Book to show that I was SAVED. No one could say I wasn't trying.

So it is difficult to explain what happened after I started attending the Methodist Sunday School. Maybe one shouldn't mix religions — the need constantly to change attitudes to dogma when going from one building to another could make one irreverent. The Methodists had a nice club on weekday evenings where I could play dominoes and work a fretsaw machine. Their Sunday School hall had windows, which I liked. So I didn't mean anything bad when I changed the words of the hymn they were singing one Sunday morning — *nobody* knew what the regular words, "loud hosannas," meant anyway.

I had always had an ear for lyrics and could repeat the words of most of the songs popular on the radio without having studied them. In those days we had a very talented disc jockey on the BBC Light Program, one Jack Jackson, whose *Record Roundup* on Saturday evenings was very popular. His manner of presentation consisted of superimposing the words of one song upon another (or following one topical song with another) to create an inappropriate and often wildly humorous situation. Perhaps I subconsciously thought that Sunday School could be improved by adopting some of his techniques.

For instance, he might combine "Steamboat Bill" with something like "I got that sinking feeling," superimposing some bubble sound effects to complete the incongruity and suggest the misfortune which befell poor Bill's steamboat. Sometimes he would merely interject more appropriate words in a song which seemed to need help, as in the old classic "The Sheik of Araby": "At night when you're asleep *without a shirt,* into your tent I'll creep *without a shirt* . . . . " I may or may not have been influenced to create my subsequent Sunday School blasphemy by such institutionalized and officially sanctioned irreverence. Anyway, I loved it.

We were standing in Sunday School singing a hymn. It required a repetitive chorus of "Loud Hosannas, Loud Hosannas to our King." It seemed to be without end — and without sense. I started thinking that it would be a much better song if it had something in it that meant something. I dug my neighbor in the ribs with my elbow and suggested "ripe bananas" in place of "loud hosannas." After all,

bananas were a great delicacy in Scotland and would probably
have been appreciated by Our King. My neighbor readily
acceded — with a little giggle — and we had hardly started
our "ripe bananas" chorus when we realized that others in
that huge room were picking it up. As we reached the end
of the hymn it was obvious that there was a struggle going
on between about fifty loud revisionists and about eighty
traditionalists — and the lady Sunday School Leader looked
as if she might have apoplexy.

A huddle of Sunday School officials convened right after
the hymn. Then the lady stood up and from the center of the
platform announced that Gordon McShean should leave the
Cathcart Road Methodist Sunday School immediately.

My neighbor, a loyal friend, got up and left with me.
That helped a lot. I might have cried otherwise. The injustice
which had been done me — condemned without opportunity
for defense — strengthened our solidarity and justified the
conspiracy we had entered into. Before we had reached the
hall exit — being watched every step of the way by these
solemn faces — we had started to giggle. As we reached the
outer exit we were helpless with laughter (it is strange how
censorious people seem to lack a sense of humor). By the
time the class was let out there were two budding revolu-
tionaries sitting outside the hall with a mock vendor's wheelbarrow offering to sell the emerging children "Ripe Bananas!"
The call was taken up by some of the other children, and I
understand that church has never been quite the same since.

It was sad that I never got to go back to the evening
sessions of dominoes and making things on the fretsaw
machine. It was all so therapeutic. All this occurred before
I became aware of the therapeutic value of a well-used curse
word, blasphemy or obscenity. A session of strong language
might have been good for the participants in that wee drama
— and a number of other people I was to meet later in life
— good, you'll remember, being a primary motive of mine.

11

Friends

The meeting of the Friends of the Library promised to be as well attended as any they had ever had. I had been given very short notice of it, and was putting in additional hours by attending (my wife had figured that I had been spending about eighty hours a week on library business in recent weeks). I was already feeling run down, but there was no way of avoiding this confrontation.

My fears about the nature of the meeting appeared to be justified when I saw the people who started to fill the room. A great number of the old stalwarts were prominent by their absence (they had received no notification of the meeting). Instead there were people I hadn't seen since the anti-smut meeting earlier in the year — some were buying "Friends" memberships as they entered the room. A friendly "Friend" — an officer who had received word of the meeting through a conversation with me that afternoon — told me that some late telephone calls he had made to members of the group confirmed that few of the library's sympathizers had been informed of the meeting. He was even sorrier to report that few of those he had contacted had been able to come because of the short notice and other commitments.

We wondered what kind of membership list had been used to bring these people to the meeting. We asked a lady sitting near us how she had learned of the meeting. She said she had been told of the meeting and invited to join the organization "some days ago." She said that the people who issued the invitation were "just acquaintances."

The meeting was being held in the library reference room, and the polished wood of the old library tables reflected the light warmly. For a moment I felt that there was little the group could do to harm me or the library in this room, almost my own creation. I had put many of the bookcases in place myself; the new reference books among the old looked bright and clean and efficient; the sense of order, and of my own control over that order, almost overwhelmed me, and I wondered if it could be felt by others in the room. But when the voice of the elderly lady who was to be presiding officer for the evening called for order, stating that the president of the organization couldn't be found, I realized that the situation could be serious.

The woman stated that it was her opinion that the Friends organization couldn't afford to have its "good name" bandied about, even by the librarian. The meeting had been called, she said, because the Friends had been associated — in print — with the "immoral and disreputable" program which the librarian had insisted on having in the library. "But it is only fair," this indignant officer went on to say, "that we give Mr. McShean a chance to explain his actions before we issue any statement on our own behalf."

A cold anger was sweeping through me as this biased introduction to my "defense" was given. I had spoken for the Friends many times in the months prior to its official formation, and could lay claim to being one of its principal founders. I had set up its model constitution so that its role in library affairs would be clear: the Friends organization was not to meddle in the administrative or policy-making affairs of the library, which were the responsibility of myself and the trustees respectively. I reminded the group of these facts in my opening remarks, and then went on to apologize for having solicited funds for their organization; " — it is unfortunate that you did not discourage my assistance earlier, when I obtained donations and new subscriptions for your organization at the library circulation desk," I said. "I had no reason to believe that the Friends would be less happy with this opportunity to obtain additional funds. You can be assured that I had no intention of giving my program any additional validity by using your name — it needs none."

"But now your budget will be in excellent shape," I continued, "since you have so many new members tonight. I hope we can count them as true Friends." Then I went on to address myself to the purpose of the meeting. "I must confess that I had not anticipated that I would hear such prejudiced opinions about a library program from the mouth of an officer of the Friends' organization." (There was a long 'Ohhh' from some of the listeners.) "A true Friend of the Library would have consulted with me about any part of the library's activities which was not understood or which was objected to — and then would have worked to have the organization assist in smoothing the library's path and spreading proper and responsible information."

There were whisperings and hostile glances everywhere I looked. I could see I was getting nowhere with the audience. I was afraid that I was getting overly defensive, but could do little to stop myself.

"As it is," I said, "I resent the manner in which this meeting was called, and I resent the implications in the remarks made by your officer. No one here knows the caliber of the materials which will be presented at the poetry reading which will be held here in the library, except for the one or two poems I mentioned to board members. And yet you all hurry here to condemn me for an 'immoral' program. Your program tonight is more despicable than anything I would be likely to present."

I was beginning to get carried away by my anger. I could feel my face flushing. "You have many people here who know nothing of the aims of this library, and many of your informed members, the ones who have concerned themselves with the library's well-being in the past, are not here. I reject your authority to call this meeting, or to consider anything I have said formally. I refuse to discuss this matter with any of you, unless I can find some members who are prepared to be objective."

With that I dramatically turned on my heel and started to walk to the door, feeling the shocked silence and the hostile stares.

"Just a minute — we didn't mean to offend you . . . " a small voice said from the audience. I suppose I had been hoping for something like that — something I could imagine as an assertion of the group's essential goodness, a sign that I had been mistaken in my judgement. Like a fool I thought that perhaps the monsters who sat around the library tables had been magically transformed. I turned back.

It only took a few minutes for me to discover my mistake in not continuing to walk out the door. I became the subject of harangues from all over the room. The poetry reading was called everything from an "ill-advised folly" to an attempt to undermine the town's youth. I was called a "newcomer" and a troublemaker, and finally was refered to as having "spread sex all over town." I objected to that charge, and got an admission from the person who had spoken that he was mistaken, " — just repeating something I'd heard!"

"You people who pretend to be moral should not be so quick to repeat what you hear," I said bitterly.

Other accusations followed apace. They were usually delivered obliquely. The disparaging statement most frequently used was a reference to my extreme youth (delivered in a paternalistic tone) — I was thirty. I had laid myself open to that kind of abuse because of a comment I had made in regard to the advanced age of the persons who were so anxious to censor the poetry of youth. It could have been funny if the purpose of the people who had called the meeting hadn't been so serious. I wondered how many of the persons in the audience realized the implications of what was going on. Did they really think that they were here simply to make the library programs "sweeter" and make the headstrong young librarian know his place? Had they any idea that their own freedom to read was at stake, and that the livelihoods of library staff members were in jeopardy? Would they understand that if I attempted to point it out?

The accusations changed to questions — perhaps they were as puzzled by my motivation as I was by theirs. The questions were meant to lead me to some admission of guilt — had I answered I would have been condemned from my own mouth. I was incensed, but I was forced to let many of these questions pass without challenge. They dealt with my personal beliefs, my religion and my life in Europe prior to coming to the United States, matters which had no relevance to the presentation of a program of poetry which we were supposed to be discussing. I continuously asserted that these matters were my own business. The meeting was becoming quite an inquisition.

I was just about at the end of my tether when a man stood up. "What is the matter, young fellow," he said, "you have an awful lot to hide, eh?"

"I don't need to stay here and be insulted by you — any of you!" I shouted. I again started to leave. "They only have one thing to vote on," a friend said, holding on to my sleeve. I paused. The chairwoman had started to call for a vote on the resolution which had been proposed. I guess I'm a sucker for meetings. I looked around me at the people who were busy shuffling papers, then sat down.

The resolution condemned programs which would not be suitable for children. I had previously tried to explain that the library could legitimately present programs geared to the adult just as it could present children's programs; I had also reiterated that the program they were discussing would be quite suitable for young people, with parental approval, and that many poems written by young people would be represented. The explanations had done no good. This resolution had been drawn up previous to the meeting and they were determined to vote on it as if I had never spoken.

Just before the vote was taken a library board member — who had sat through the meeting in silence (only one other board member was present, and she too had kept silent) — asked if the company would not instead approve a resolution referring the matter to the board. "You can be assured the library board will do the correct thing," she said. There was no support forthcoming for her suggestion, and the group went on to complete the vote, scribbling their *yeas* and *nays* on little slips of paper and folding them up.

The motion, it should be mentioned, also disassociated the Friends group from the proposed program and "any similar." It passed with an overwhelming majority.

The one officer who had been friendly to me now called a point of order, asking that it be ascertained that a quorum was present. The chair boldly disallowed his request and adjourned the meeting.

Within a few moments the library had started to empty. Everyone left in a quiet and orderly manner. There was very little conversation. It was quite a contrast to the mood of the meeting previous to the vote.

As they were leaving the treasurer (who had seemingly been invited to attend because she issued the membership cards) sidled up to me where I was standing with the other friendly officer. She was obviously scared. "Mr. McShean," she said, "I have the membership records here and I checked to see if there was a quorum this evening. Even with the new people — a lot of them didn't pay to join — there was no quorum. Lots of regulars didn't get word of the meeting. And a lot of people who spoke against you weren't members." She looked around with the same frightened look in her eyes. "I told Mr. _____ (another officer) that there wasn't a quorum and that the vote was no good. He told me I'd better forget that information or I'd be sorry!"

The other officer, a young man, had been listening intently. He gave me a quick glance and turned briskly to the door where the woman who had presided was exiting. "Don't sweat it!" he said to the concerned treasurer as he went.

Within a few moments he was back. "I got the whole bunch of them outside," he said. "You know the old lady prides herself in having been a parliamentarian. I told her and the others that if the word got about that they had passed that resolution I would expose this as a rigged meeting!"

"How did they take it?" the treasurer asked.

"Quietly," he said. Then he turned to me, smiling. "Just consider that this whole evening never happened, Gordon."

June was standing next to me, trying to force a smile. I knew how she felt. The trouble was that we knew it all had happened.

12

Rumors

The furor showed no sign of abating. Rumors were flying all over town. It didn't seem to matter that the rumors often contradicted each other. There was little concern for facts, as can be seen from the circumstance that no one had asked me what poems I intended to read since the matter had become public (if one excludes the expressions of general interest made by board members at their earlier meeting).

One of the rumors was concerned with my display of "psychedelic" newspapers, apparently, but the story was so twisted by the time it reached me that the source is only conjecture on my part. The story could have been manufactured maliciously without any basis in fact. It was said that I had posted materials "exposing the sex lives of priests" on bulletin boards all over the children's department (we only had one bulletin board in the children's department, and that was devoted to official announcements). When I received that information I was stung into saying to my informant "But — I didn't know priests had sex lives!"

Another rumor, contradicting the other, had a little more basis in fact; this had it that I insisted on keeping children from the poetry reading program because I knew the materials I would be reading would be "so filthy." A number of people were crediting both stories. "Surely," I asked those who repeated the rumors to me, "I would have been consistent in attempting to debauch or to protect the minds of the children?" They simply laughed.

I was angered because the "enemy," the censorious element of the community, was making use of my concession — the agreement to limit children's attendance — as a base from which to attack me. It was similar to an attack upon me which had been made from the floor of the city council chamber, so it was a well-traveled assumption. It could be presumed to be part of the blueprint of their attack. It made me wary of ever considering a concession to such people again.

Another rumor — that the civic groups in town who donated money to support special library purposes, such as the purchase of new encyclopedias, would cease to do so — was partially confirmed when a representative of one of the clubs paid me a visit and said he was sorry but they just didn't have the money this year . . . . I was left wondering how many other clubs would restrict their support without extending us the courtesy of an excuse.

My staff was a good source of community information. "Did you hear about the sermon yesterday?" one staff member asked. Monday morning is not one of my best times, so I grunted that I had not.

"It seems you were condemned to burn in hell for all eternity by one of our compassionate Baptist ministers," she said cheerfully. "It seems they are determined to get even your immortal soul. How does that grab you?"

I had said previously, when I had heard that the Friends organization wanted to condemn me, "But they can't do that." Now I heard myself say "They can't do that!" again.

"With God, anything is possible," said my staff member with a friendly smile.

We had been receiving anonymous telephone calls, some

serious and some abusive, both at the library and at home. I was in constant touch with board members, who were as helpful as possible. Even those members who had not agreed that we should continue with the presentation of poetry sympathized with us now. Some of them had received calls too, but none reported the viciousness which characterized our calls. The board was committed to the program, dedicated to preserving its own prerogatives in guiding the library, and naturally concerned about threats to the staff and the library's operation.

I was especially concerned about the threats which were being received by June at home while I was at work. We had some suspicions about the identity of the callers, nothing more. There were at least two callers who had taken to calling us in the middle of the night. Unfortunately we were unable to make a firm identification of any speaker so that we might have done something. The communications which bothered us most weren't the anonymous ones — when we were able to put a tentative name to those who abused us the threats seemed much more specific.

I received word that I could expect the library would no longer receive a donation from another civic organization because of one of its officers. This man was well known to me and I was surprised that he would use his influence for such a purpose. He had had opportunities to discuss our programs. His action would harm the library, although it would do little to influence a course towards censorship. My informant gave a knowing smile. "Did you, by any chance, get an abusive telephone call shortly after supper last night?"

We had had a particularly nasty call that evening — my wife had taken it — and I told him this.

"Someone else who was with him last night told me he made a call, and I thought it might have been to you."

I called my wife immediately and asked her if she thought the voice on the telephone had sounded like Mr. _____. She said it might have been, but she was shocked that anyone of his stature would stoop to such a thing. She didn't want to believe it. Then she said "But we had other calls this morning, darling — I thought your call might be them again — it wasn't anything important, just the usual swearing and telling us to get out of town." She obviously wasn't going to let me know she was bothered.

I asked her if she'd like to have the telephone company clear our calls, or if she'd rather not answer the telephone until I came home, but she would have none of that.

Later the same day I had a serious telephone call from a man I didn't know but who identified himself as a principal in a school in the community. He said that he had called to find out if what he had heard about me was true: did I really intend to read the works of living poets from California? I assured him that I did.

His tone was quite hostile. "How can a person responsible for part of our children's education, as you as librarian are, be so irresponsible as to present the materials of poets still living?" he shouted over the phone.

"You can't be serious — " I said.

"We school people have learned that a poet's worth is never known until he is dead," he went on. "You should take some advice from us, who know about this, and stop this nonsense about intellectual freedom, spreading this filth. Our young people — "

"Hey, wait a minute," I interrupted. "I got one of my degrees in English, although you might never know it, and I know there were all kinds of poets recognized as being great during their lifetimes — what kind of school did you go to?"

"We wait until they are dead!"

"Then all I can say is that I am glad I have no children who have to depend on you for an education!" I said.

The letters to the editor column of the local newspaper, the *Roswell Daily Record*, had by now run into the dozens on the issue of the poetry reading. Some were pro and some were con. The pressures had grown to such an extent that I decided I would have to write a letter myself to answer some of the charges and clear up some of the misinformation.

My letter appeared just two days before the reading was scheduled. It was accompanied by the following letter, which deserved more attention than my own. I had not known that it was being submitted.

To the People of Roswell:

Conservatism, my friends, is fine. But when it acts as a cover for sheer ignorance, it becomes dangerous.

Concerning your disapproval of "hippie poetry" — since when is the quality of poetry judged by the poet's social status? If good social behavior was any criterion for good poetry, Lord Byron would have died a nameless debauchee, and Shelley's atheism would have doomed him to obscurity.

Mr. Truett Worley refers to "a group of non-productive LSD addicts" in his letter of September 10. (First of all, Mr. Worley, there is no such thing as an LSD addict. LSD is non-addictive.) But aside from that, how can you call hippies non-productive? Your letter was written to condemn the poetry which they have produced. In your years as an English teacher at Roswell High and an upstanding citizen of Roswell, what, Mr. Worley, have you produced?

And you, Mrs. Spradling, how much hippie poetry did you read before condemning them so vigorously? and what are the "decent things in life" to which you refer? Perhaps you mean those outstanding citizens on the public library's board of directors who voted to provide the library with hippie poetry. Surely you don't think that Mr. McShean could make it available without the board's approval? But of course, he has a beard, so he makes a marvelous scapegoat.

If it is the hippies you disapprove of, that's fine. But don't reject their poetry because you disagree with their ideas. That type of condemnation is the result of extremely primitive reasoning. It is the logical fallacy of *argumentum ad hominum*, or rejecting the principle because of personal prejudice against the man who presents it.

To the Roswell Public Library we say "Welcome to the Twentieth Century" Sincerely,
Kathleen Wiggins
Elaine Wiggins

This letter of support from members of the famous Wiggins family (they are well known artists in the Southwest, but I had never met them) was a great boost to me. My own letter seemed less necessary, but there it was, too. I had written:

Dear Editor:

I only wanted to read poetry. Poetry, that's all. I've read lots of poetry in Roswell — had a hundred fifty people at one reading earlier this year. People seem to get pleasure from my readings. We have nearly a hundred reservations for my Thursday reading now.

That is why I am disturbed about the reaction of people in Roswell to the latest part of the reading program: "hippie" poetry — contemporary poetry if you like — poetry meaningful to people in our day, not material from two hundred-odd years ago, such as I'd read before. Why are people afraid of it? Don't tell me people expect me to make converts for hippie-ism?

What makes otherwise responsible people make judgments without investigation? No one even asked me what was in the poetry I would read.

What makes "solid citizens" write abusive letters to the newspaper, claim our freedoms are being threatened and that we must therefore deny these same freedoms, make anonymous phone calls, and threaten to coerce public officials to halt financial support by civic groups? All of these things have happened to us in Roswell during the past week.

If I was wrong in asking that children be accompanied by adults to the program, I'm sorry. But we do have children's programs. Why not an adult one? I'm inclined to think, however, that the furor might have been even greater had I not made such a rule.

Would you, for example, want your child to hear me read the poetry of the Old Testament in the Song of Solomon? The library has books for adults, and hopefully will be able to present cultural programs aimed at them.

Presuming for a moment that some of the people who have protested this reading knew what I had chosen to read (as I've said, none asked me), would they then be within their rights to ask for a ban on it? No one has yet accused me to my face of being, like Socrates, bent on corrupting the young. Therefore we will presume my program to be purely a cultural one. Can the public choose to hear one part of a cultural program and not another?

I say the means are at hand for those who are so well informed about hippies, or Robert Burns, or Browning, to keep from hearing their writings read: they need not attend. But they have no right to dictate their prejudices to others. As I mentioned, we have nearly a hundred firm reservations made for the reading and many other expressions of interest. We can only take between fifty and sixty in the library comfortably — we have taken the names of the "extras" and have promised a second reading soon if the demand is still with us.

I am gratified that there is so much interest in the poetry. It shows that there are some people in Roswell interested in knowing about one facet of our alienated society — the poetry of our young people. I'll be most happy to listen to complaints, comments — even praise — about the reading. . . after it has been read and people know what they are talking about.

It has given me great pleasure, under the direction of the board, to present cultural books, displays and programs to the people of Roswell. I am told that it has been appreciated by some.

Gordon McShean

After the letters were published we all sat back and waited for additional reactions. We wished the reading was over and done with.

Again, the rumor mill was working. One of the staff members was sitting in the basement drinking coffee with me, and a couple of the high-school-age children of staff members were sitting listening. "The grapevine has it that you are arranging for a whole bunch of hippies to come to Roswell so that you will have a sympathetic audience for your readings," the staff member said.

"They will be out of luck when they get here," I said, "'cos I don't have any reservations left."

"The grapevine is a little less definite about this, but you are supposedly arranging for them to come and sleep in sleeping bags in your living room, or to camp out in your back yard. And your last trip to El Paso was to get them some cheap liquor to drink."

We sat in silence for a while. "Do you think they'd drink — shouldn't I have bought some pot instead?" I asked. The school kids giggled.

The staff member went on: "There was one other rumor — it seems that some kid was down here late one evening working on an art project (you know those art books), and he had hardly been here any length of time when he saw a nude."

The children giggled some more, and then one of them said something which made the whole day seem worth while:

"Don't be silly! Who would want to look at a nude librarian?"

13

Bibliosexuality

There have been a number of occasions when I've asked myself why a young man would do such an odd thing as to become a librarian? It is the kind of question a mortician might ask himself about his career if he had a sense of humor. A sensitive person survives in the straight-faced professions only by developing a healthy skepticism towards the seriousness which his or her colleagues use to endow their usually boring and removed-from-life routines with an appearance of dignity.

Not that there isn't something serious about the task of handing over library information which may be used to influence world affairs — or about preparing somebody's corpse for the hole. But the serious things in life are the things which must be viewed from a properly human perspective, and the only quality unique to humans in all the animal world is a sense of humor. The librarian (or the mortician) perceptive enough to ask himself how he came to be what he is would need a sense of humor.

Library work is notoriously low-paid work, so there is little likelihood that individuals would choose the profession — as morticians might — to "make a killing" (if you will excuse the expression). There are those who are librarians because they obviously like quiet, intellectually prestigious office work with little responsibility. Then there are those who simply love books, who take the job to get near the objects of their misplaced love. Unless they are able to develop their sense of humanity to compensate for the weakness which led them to this, these people discredit the profession.

The persons who love books have never been properly analyzed, I feel. There are many people outside the library profession — compulsive paperback buyers included (although they lack the fellowship and the glamor of the beautiful, hide-bound book people) — who suffer from the same compulsion. I am tempted, while examining the many reasons which might impel a person to devote his life to books, to postulate a theory of compulsive *bibliosexuality*.

How many people were fated to spend the first years of their sexual lives dependent for gratification upon the pages of an open book instead of the comfort and ease of open arms and open pajama fronts? It is a commentary upon the limitations of this system we call *civilization*. And how many such people would now be as happy to go to bed with a good book as with a human sex partner? If there is any substance to the concept of bibliosexuality it will not only explain some of the aberrations in the behavior of librarians, it will throw some light upon the existence of the many other strange persons who can be observed in the public library from time to time.

If there is such an affliction as bibliosexuality (who would ever have thought of book lovers as deviates?) be assured that I am not going to call for some major program to isolate the victims from the causative agents and contaminants. Such a course would be useless, since we have observed that it takes very little — in a censorship ridden society — to inspire sexual thoughts from an expurgated page.

If bibliosexuality exists then we must promote an awareness of the condition and a sympathy for its victims. We need to recognize the need for the habit to be continuously fed and the danger inherent in withdrawal — the addict will find gratification somewhere. It is an argument for better and more complete libraries. Perhaps that's why I became a librarian, to serve the afflicted?

If bibliosexuality is eventually discovered to be a condition affecting society in general, and subsequently becomes a problem (for instance, if interpersonal relations descend to the level where the highest expression of concern is a gift of a sexy book and the population drops drastically), we may have to do something to avert the occurrence of book/sex addiction in the young in order to continue the race. Then we may have to establish institutions dedicated to real sex instead of the vicarious kind. I can't help thinking that work in such an institution would be even more gratifying than work in a library. Perhaps I was born too soon.

Being an advocate of living life to the fullest, I have examined myself for the taint of bibliosexuality and found that there is only a slight dependency. I enjoy a good book, but reject the epithet of book lover (I can't even remember authors' names — and I became a librarian!).

If I am not dependent upon books and the other media, why then do I take such pains to confront the censors? And why *did* I become a librarian? It is difficult for me to discover a reason. When I asked a young female librarian — who had no sexual hang-ups that I could discover — why she had become a librarian she answered "Perhaps I did it for a giggle."

I can't think that that would have been my reason — I haven't giggled very much since becoming a librarian. But I do know one thing: being a mortician never appealed to me.

14

Live Poetry

Janice Lucas was almost as odd a character as myself — she had grown up in the Southwest, but had traveled extensively in Europe and elsewhere, even having worked on a kibbutz in Israel. She had had some library experience in London, and I jumped at the chance of hiring her to help in our library. She was pretty, and hardly out of her teens. She had acquired a delightful English accent, and absolutely refused to drop back into the Southern-style drawl she had grown up with. She was thoroughly competent in performing her task as library assistant to young people.

It was only natural that I would ask her to assist in the presentation of the poems. I don't think I was surprised when she said she'd be delighted.

"I don't have to stay here, Mr. McShean," she said, "so I have nothing to lose. I am thinking of going out to the Coast anyway. I think Roswell needs a program like this, regardless of what is read — the important thing is that they learn that other things are happening in the world."

I had steadfastly refused to make a decision on what would be read until the day before the presentation, but now that I had an ally it was easy to sit down and pick the pieces that each of us would read. We had to admit that our final choice was quite mild. We decided that we were better to choose controversiality of content rather than blow everything on a few taboo words. The message was what was important. So we ended up with some very well-written pieces opposing the war, describing the sex act, and praising the joys of release through psychedelic drugs — mixed with some quite harmless humorous pieces. There were very few "nasty" words.

Then we planned the presentation. It was difficult, since we had to put a dictionary stand on top of a library table in order to make some kind of stage, and then we had to figure out a safe way to get up and down as our poems alternated. We had incense and candles to set the mood. But the setting was a problem. The rows and rows of antique library chairs destroyed the relaxed mood we were trying to create. The best we could say for it was that it was indeed "funky." We had no alternative other than to give in to the conditions which the building and furnishings imposed on us. We thought we might improve things by agreeing to dress as casually as possible, and by putting psychedelic posters on the dictionary stand to brighten the set.

It isn't really strange that the poetry we would read that evening would leave little impression in our minds — even though most of it was very good. The important thing was in giving the reading against all opposition. The material could have been gibberish. People will perhaps stop asking "what was the material they wanted to ban?" if they once understand that doing it — putting it on — making it available — is of far more importance to the censor and the opposition than any one piece of writing.

We had our poetry in bundles, our candles and incense ready in saucers in the staff room and our dictionary stand placed solidly on the table. We were ready.

Board members and friends ran a shuttle service from the city hall a few blocks away where the council was meeting. The meeting had been scheduled an hour before our reading was to start, and reports came back that all hell was breaking loose. They were threatening to close us down, have us arrested, and all kinds of other things.

A number of people came to me and asked if I wouldn't reconsider. It was not too late to halt the destruction of the library, they said, if I would only change my mind and call the thing off. We still had half an hour. I said I had to risk the structure rather than risk the basic principles upon which it operated — but I think that was beyond their comprehension. "You still have twenty minutes — call if off!" We brought out the candles and the incense. "You still have fifteen minutes!" Then people came in and began to take their seats. It was too late to call it off. My self-appointed advisers gave up on me.

Hair-raising tales of the politics going on at the city council meeting were brought back to us. The council had backed down on its threat to cut funds from the library budget. Instead there was a move afoot to see that I was fired (I knew that the appointment of the head librarian was the board's prerogative, not that of the city council; I had confidence they would stand firm).

There was a story that the city police department had been authorized to place a padlock on the library doors and permit no one to enter or leave until the time of the reading had passed. The only evidence we had of police awareness of our existence was in the frequency with which police cars crawled past our front door.

There were a few cars parked in the street outside the library with men sitting in them, and no one knew who they were. There had been some threats of rocks being thrown through the library windows if the program continued, and even a wild rumor of a firebomb. We did not feel reassured.

Soon the library was filled, and there wasn't any evidence of support from the hip community (whatever or wherever that might be). It was one of the straightest-looking crowds I'd seen. But we had an illusion to create, and we set about creating it, trying to bring the audience with us. We dimmed the lights, lit the candles and incense, and then I got up on the table top, behind the dictionary stand with its brightly colored poster, and waited for silence in order to begin. Within a few seconds you could have heard a pin drop.

It was a harrowing task, but I began a poem. There was silence, except for an occasional cough. The poem that I read was my own — although I did not inform the audience of the authorship. It was called *Small Town*, and had been written just a few days previous to the reading. I read:

> Fear   Hate   Gossip
> An American small town
>   keeps itself
>   Itself
>   keeps
>   keeps itself righteous
>   by such things
>
> Using such respected weapons
>   and an occasional
>   anonymous letter
>   and phone call
>   about wicked things
>   learned in the dark
>   with the smell of incense
>   making the air smell clean
> (half discerned things
>   or things learned
>   by righteous intuition)

they breathe
with breath made clean
by sterile mouthwash
that "these things should be
brought to
LIGHT"

Halo light shines
on all the half truths
righteous prejudices
as the townspeople
put their heads together
to decide punishments for transgressors
nonconformists
those who L O V E
Halo light illuminates their decisions
as they put their
close cropped heads
together
and pierce the dark with sermons
social ostracism
financial ruin
STARVATION
JAIL
quiet violence
HELL
All these threats, WEAPONS
are used
used
used
used
abused
until those without the halo
wither   flee   die
or repent

Had God lived here
had God
    ever been
   been
   HERE
He would have denied His Son
   long hair
    and freedom
   to talk of love
    and sandals
Had God lived
   HERE
He would have denied His Son
   LOVE
for fear of what the townspeople
   might do to Him

When I finished there was enthusiastic applause from a portion of the audience, with a more grudging response coming from the rest. I did not elaborate on the meanings of the poem, feeling that the poem had justified itself.

My next poem was from the Haight-Ashbury and was to be about drugs. I allowed myself the luxury of citing a couple of authorities — whose works could be consulted in the library — on the effects of LSD and pot. I said that they had stated there was so little scientific information available on the effects of these drugs that we should suspend judgment until more was known. "We can't be sure that LSD does split genes," I said, "but I'm sure there are people in Roswell who would be happy to have an expanded market for the jeans we produce here." (Roswell had a Levi factory.) That got a laugh.

From then on the going was comparatively easy. I read the poem and handed the podium ever to Janice. She did her bit very effectively, got a good response, and handed it back to me, and so we continued the evening.

At the end of the program there was loud applause, with a few persons notably silent and disapproving. I think we were more relieved to find that the program had gone off without incident than appreciative of the applause, but it was nice anyway.

A board member came up to me as he was leaving and said that he had enjoyed the program, although poetry wasn't of much interest to him. "I thought your explanations of the poetry and the reasons you gave for the attitudes that came out of the poems were helpful," he said. He stopped, looked at me a little sheepishly, then handed me a piece of paper. "I hope you don't mind, but I was doing a statistical count of the bad words you used," he said.

I looked at the piece of paper and saw written on it:
HELL IIII,   WHORE I,   DAMN IIIIII,   FART I
"You mean you counted . . . ?" I said.

"It was for your own protection!"

I looked at him with some amazement on my face as he left the building smiling. I was surprised that he should have considered counting the words at all. I was even more surprised that I hadn't said anything worse than that — I hadn't been conscious of cleaning it up to that extent.

I found my wife ushering people out of the library and took her aside to show her the piece of paper.

June started to chuckle as she saw what was written on the paper.

I was still a little indignant. "Shit," I said, "I wonder what he'd have said if he'd known that one of the hells was my own?"

June laughed.

15

Resigning Myself

The day after the poetry reading the *Roswell Daily Record* carried this report:

HIPPIE POETRY IS READ DESPITE FUROR

No evidence of the storm raging over the use of the Roswell Public Library for the reading of hippie poetry appeared as poetry was read quietly and dramatically last night in the library by Head Librarian Gordon McShean and Miss Janice Lucas, a library employee.

There was no furor over the fact that less than an hour before the poetry reading started, the Roswell City Council in a recessed meeting had changed its mind after voting to cut off all financial support to the library if the hippie poetry reading took place as scheduled in the public library.

Aldermen and library board members were discussing the situation as the witching hour of eight o'clock neared. Feelings were strong, pro and con, when the city council voted to take "police action," as it was described by one alderman, against the library through economic pressure and then decided that this was going too far as tempers cooled a bit and raw nerves were soothed.

NO BAD LANGUAGE

There was no bad language or four-letter words in the poetry read by the librarian and one of his assistants. There were reports beforehand that there might be. Library board member Penrod Toles told the city council that there was never any intention of having poetry read that would shock sensibilities. "I can assure you," he told the council, "there will be no four-letter words used."

The poetry came from several sources, including "Hello," by J.D. Whitney and a newspaper described as an "underground newspaper" published in the Chicago area.

Poems such as the following from "Hello" brought laughs from the audience as candles burned and incense permeated the Library air:

MAXIM 27

If I were
you

it would
in short be

a phenomenon
most difficult

to explain
to my wife

We were very happy about the fair coverage the newspaper had given the whole matter. We hoped it would smooth things over. We had promised ourselves that after the reading was over it would calm down and we would be able to relax, but we couldn't have been more wrong. Things got progressively worse.

Fortunately Janice, who had done such a nice job of reading the poetry with me, found a reason to go to California immediately and did not suffer any indignities. But my wife and I began to feel persecuted as each new day brought an additional insult of some kind.

June had been very active in the Women's Club until a few weeks previous to the reading. She had spent almost a whole week on arranging a sale for the club, often coming home late at night exhausted by her efforts — efforts which eventually brought a considerable amount of money into the club coffers. Now she found that she was being ostracized by the majority of the club members. This made me very angry, as I knew how hard she had worked and how much the social life of the club meant to her. It was fortunate that she had other interests — involving the special educational programs for Spanish-speaking youth — to keep her busy and make her feel that her efforts were worthwhile. But I was angry about the attitudes of her so-called friends in the Women's Club, especially since there was no justice in blaming her for my actions.

We were brought even closer together by the circumstances. Whenever we had a few hours to spare we found ourselves driving to Lincoln, Santa Fe, El Paso, Carlsbad or Ruidoso, all the places that were close enough to visit but far enough away so that we wouldn't be recognized and have to wonder if the persons looking at us approved or disapproved of us. We escaped whenever we could.

In Roswell I don't think it would be an exaggeration to say that I was known by sight to at least twenty thousand people because of my frequent participation in community events, my appearances on television (I did children's programs, a heart fund panel talk, etc.), my parts in the community theatre, my frequent speeches to civic organizations and visits to classrooms — and my position as librarian. At first it had been exciting to know that I was well known and well received. But now, as the nasty telephone calls continued, as the rumors spread and developed in new, malign ways, we began to fear that many of the people who recognized us looked at us askance.

We could take some consolation from the fact that librarians all over the state had expressed their sympathy over what had happened, and had sent statements endorsing my way of handling the matter. The library board itself seemed to be largely happy with what I had done. And members of the staff were almost entirely in accord with my actions. We found ourselves depending more and more on these people to boost our morale.

But as things grew progressively worse our friends failed to appreciate what was happening. They did not see our need. With the reading over the crisis was over as far as they were concerned. We could no longer communicate our pain.

Our theatrical friends found the whole situation laughable. I had played a supporting role — as a psychiatrist — in Horine's comedy *Me and Thee* earlier in the year, and had been nominated for an award. As far as they were concerned I should have been more worried about getting that award and preparing for the upcoming season in the theatre. They appointed me to the board of directors. To them the reading thing had grown to be a *bore.*

They did help us keep our minds off our worries to a certain extent. June helped backstage, and I agreed to direct an English comedy for later in the season, reasoning that some kind of normalizing influence would have touched our lives by then. I could foresee problems in casting the Cockneys and the Yorkshiremen I needed, given the Texas and Louisiana accents of our local talent. But all of that seemed terribly far in the future. I was still grappling with the elementary problems of keeping the library running.

Library routine had changed drastically, so that a great deal of time was spent in defensive preparation. Some of our staff members could remember the threats of the early sixties when right-wing extremists had caused a concern for the safety of everyone who worked in the library. I arranged frequent meetings with staff members — using contrived reasons — in order to try to keep staff morale from plummeting. It was difficult to make light of our problems and act light-hearted at these meetings, but it was necessary to do so.

My paperback project seemed to be drawing a lot of fire from the people who were concerned about our library as a source of contamination for the minds of youth. We were constantly scared, it seemed, and I started asking myself if the whole thing was worth it.

Everyone outside the library who supported us continued to take everything very calmly. We were being threatened every day, but their reaction when we told them of the incidents was always: "They are nuts — don't pay any attention to them!" The telephone calls continued, and I was hearing slanders against my wife as well as myself. I consulted an American Civil Liberties Union lawyer, but he said there was no legal action we could take unless I could *prove* that some person had been maliciously circulating a slander. I asked a number of people if they would testify to what they had heard from certain sources and they declined to do so.

I had been receiving statements of support from members of the library profession, and now I started to receive endorsements from the professional organizations. I couldn't help feeling that some of this new support would have changed things if it had come before the reading, and that such endorsements were easy to make now that I had come out of the confrontation — from a professional standpoint at least — smelling like a rose. When I mentioned this to fellow librarians, however, they rebuked me. "You can't expect organizations to act in a hurry, you know. They have to be sure of what they are doing." I had to presume that the rule went for all organizations except the John Birch Society and the Citizens for Decent Literature.

I was being invited to give readings here, there and everywhere. But I had so far refused to even consider scheduling the second reading which had been promised to those who had failed to get reservations for the first. I told myself that I had not given in to the pressures, that I was simply holding myself in reserve until a time would appear propitious. Holding the readings again would cost me more than I could afford to expend in personal reserves of energy.

On one of our trips away from town I did give an impromptu reading of *Small Town* at the Chase Mansion, a coffee house in El Paso. Here university students were enjoying some short-lived freedom (the coffee house was under such constant attack from university authorities and other "straight" influences in the town that we wondered about its continued existence each time we visited El Paso).

The students viewed themselves as a haven of rationality in a vast territory of reaction. They were delighted by our appearance at their coffee house, and by my poem, and expressed amazement that people like us could live in such a place as Roswell, New Mexico.

A student told us a story about an event which he had heard about in nearby Arizona. A hippie family (man, woman and infant) had been suspended from the edge of a cliff with ropes by farmers "for suspected sheep stealing." They had been there for many hours before they were rescued. Their ordeal was supposedly based upon an old Indian tradition for punishment. The reason given for their victimization, it seemed, was that they had been observed borrowing books on leather work from the local library.

I experienced a chill as I heard the student tell the story and add the statement implicating the library. But there was comfort in being able to talk to people who sympathized with our purposes. We told them that we found it amazing that such students could exist in El Paso, Texas. But I consoled myself with the thought that reactionary societies always produce enclaves of persons concerned for humanity. The question remained, however: how much repression did it take for such enclaves to become viable forces of resistance?

Back in Roswell what rankled most were the remarks made by members of the city council in the heat of "debate," particularly the remarks of the mayor. These remarks ranged from the call for me to be fired to the mayor's "He's got a beard and he's a Buddhist — you can tell what kind of man he is from that!" Most of the comments about me had been extremely personal and had little or nothing to do with my performance as a librarian. It had all been said without any attempt to allow me to defend myself, while I was busy with library duties.

Members of the board continued to take the remarks lightly, although many had been entered into the official record and reported in the local press. Even a second threat to take the library's funds away unless I "behaved" was taken as empty rhetoric. When I told board members that I could not operate under that kind of coercion I was told that I was making a mountain out of a mole hill.

I felt that any new slander could provide council members with the excuse to raise more hell, and I (and the library) would again be in trouble.

One night June and I discussed our predicament into the wee hours of the morning. We decided that there was no point in staying with the library if the board was going to leave us so vulnerable to attack by members of the city council. A proper library board should act as a buffer to shield employees from the political pressures of local government (among other things), and they were not doing that. I stayed up most of the night to type out my resignation, and early next morning I submitted it in confidence to members of the board. I wrote:

Honorable members of the Board of Trustees
of the Roswell Public Library:

It is with regret, considering the support I have received from the board and various responsible members of the community, that I feel constrained to submit my resignation as head librarian of the Roswell Public Library.

I feel that neither the board nor the staff of the library can
operate an efficient library facility under [a threat]. No proper
book selection or arrangement of cultural programs can be
made whilst such a threat to withdraw our financial support
remains in effect . . . . Is the future of the library to be
threatened each time there is a hysterical outburst over
nothing, as in the case of the "hippie" poetry reading . . . ?
The administrator of the library must have the authority —
and the confidence of his superiors — to present the best
of literature to the public. This authority has been under-
mined by the statements of the mayor and the actions of the
city council.

I then went on to agree that our general performance was
below standard because of inadequate funding. The council
had not supported past budget requests. I went on:

I am required by professional obligation and personal conviction to uphold the freedom of intellectual inquiry. This is
a cause and a freedom which more people in Roswell are
going to have to stand up for. [The mayor had stated publicly
that "McShean overlooks nothing to exploit 'his cause'. . . "].

It has been a pleasure working for such an enlightened
group of individuals as this board has shown itself to be.
I regret that the board has not been permitted to continue
its jurisdiction for the benefit of the people of Roswell,
which it has shown itself eminently capable of doing. I
therefore submit my resignation.

Sincerely,

(signed) Gordon McShean

It took more than a week for the board to get together to discuss my resignation, and during that week my wife and I were on tenterhooks imagining the publicity which might result and the possibility of additional attacks being made on us.

When the board finally discussed it and refused the resignation I was quite taken aback. We hadn't even entertained the idea that they might refuse to accept it. I was particularly chagrined when it appeared that one or two of the board members seemed to have a suspicion that my resignation hadn't been serious in the first place — that I had expected to have it refused.

But although they refused the resignation they did undertake to approach the mayor and the city council about the continued threat to library funding. They set up a committee for an approach to the council and to undertake the matter of the mayor's personal remarks about me. Therefore, being a reasonable man (and somewhat confused) I agreed to stay in Roswell.

When I told June she, too, was confused. Suddenly our avenue of escape was closed. We were again vulnerable.

16

Strays

The antagonism that we had felt before continued. Some of the harassments seem petty now, but at the time they seemed serious enough.

The State Fair was scheduled for Roswell. I had always considered public relations one of my strong points, and was anxious to obtain a booth for the library at the fair. The library had never been represented before. For weeks I called the responsible fair officer to get a booth. I finally gave up the attempt after one telephone conversation, shortly after the poetry reading, when he asked me who I thought I was, " — asking for special privileges?"

I knew that each year booths were put aside by authorities for non-profit and public service organizations. The special privilege I was seeking was routine. The man's attitude was outrageous. But I had decided I hadn't the strength to fight every dragon that breathed fire on me — it was easier to give in.

We were surprised when we visited the fair the day after it opened and found a large, prominent booth marked ROS-WELL PUBLIC LIBRARY. It was empty. People were passing with raised eyebrows, remarking on the wasted space.

A quick visit to the fair office brought the information that the booth had been assigned some weeks previously, and that the officer who had been nasty to me on the telephone had been responsible for informing me that we had a booth. I immediately asked to see him. After a lengthy wait he arrived at the office and I got another dose of unpleasantness. He yelled that if I had no interest in seeing that I had a booth, it sure as hell wasn't his goddamn responsibility to chase after me to see that I was informed.

I reminded him of my numerous telephone calls and his remarks that I could not be offered "special privileges."

"You're goddamn right — you should be damn lucky you got a booth — you got no right to bitch!" he said.

There were a number of people in the office who were obviously embarrassed by the scene the man was causing. He had just come from the rodeo and was clearly bursting with cowboy-identification aggressiveness.

"I don't have to listen to that kind of talk," I said, being inwardly offended but perversely rejoicing at the opportunity to appear righteous for once. I picked up my exhibitor's passes from a solicitous secretary and marched out of the office. I almost laughed when I realized that my comment had some irony in it. The man was probably acting in this way because of the language he imagined I had used at the poetry reading! But my anger at the treatment I had received was seething, nevertheless.

That whole evening was spent in digging materials out of storage in the library to make up the display. My wife — a great worker — helped. There were still five fair days that we could take advantage of.

We took some of our large print books for those who might have difficulty reading, and we took a load of our newer children's picture books. We had a microfilm reader and some rolls of film of the *New York Times*. People would be able to see the new services we offered. We could also issue library cards at the booth.

We spent many hours getting the display materials together and putting them in place. We also had to arrange for library employees and sympathetic volunteers to staff the booth. June and I covered it for the first day just to see that everything went smoothly. It appeared that we had left no loose ends, and the public responded with friendly curiosity. There were no questions about the recent controversy, just innocent remarks and inquiries about the library services represented at the booth. The children enjoyed looking at filmed newspapers through our microfilm reader, and the adults enjoyed looking at the children's picture books. We issued a number of library cards. We were both very tired — but happy — when we closed the booth that night.

When I got to the library early the next morning, however, I found the library staff in a frenzy. They had tried to reach me at the fair by telephone, but had been unable to get anyone to transmit a message to me from the fair's office to the booth. I had returned home too late in the evening for them to risk bothering me. They told me that the Daughters of the American Revolution (popularly known as the DAR) had come to the library with many complaints, apparently fully aware that I was not in the building. This was the group which had previously complained when the library had purchased materials in Spanish, saying "these Mexicans pay only a small proportion of the city taxes — why should we spend our book money on getting reading material for them?" I had given them short shrift, telling them they should be ashamed of themselves for not having a concern for people who were less fortunate than themselves — particularly as these people had settled the New Mexico territory long before any of the DAR's forebears even knew of its existence.

Now the DAR had taken revenge. Their members had

marched into the library *en masse*, had harangued the staff members on duty, and then had set up a work team to remove the many books on genealogy which the library had received from the group over the years on "permanent loan." These were the books the members of the group used to trace their lineage back to approved historical antecedents — they were seldom used by anyone excepting the group members themselves and an occasional Mormon. We probably should have been charging them for storage costs all these years.

The staff member I had left in charge hadn't known what to do. One of the grand dames had said something about not maintaining *their* collection in an "unAmerican" library after one of the clerks at the desk asked if they weren't going to check the books out. There had been a regular parade of old ladies in and out of the library, with a number of big shiny cars outside, their trunks weighted down with dusty volumes.

The "raid" was really an illegal action since no arrangements had been made with the library for the release of the books from our custody, but there was little I could do without inviting another public scandal.

We were soon to discover that there had been a loose end at the display in the state fair too. One of the Daughters of the American Revolution had mentioned to a staff member that there were materials in the library belonging to their sister organization the Daughters of the American Colonists. These materials included the microfilm reader that the library had been using to scan its files of the *New York Times*. Within a day the display at the fair found itself with files of microfilm and no reader to provide access to them.

The fair was a success to us, nevertheless. We had materials showing the statistics of library support in Roswell as compared to other places in the state, and I am sure a great many people were made aware of the library's problems who would never have approached us directly at the library. We issued a goodly number of library cards, and soon the bearers of these "fair" cards were showing up at the library and checking out books.

The booth also kept our minds off our own personal problems for a while. We had decided to try to sell our home, and we were faced with the prospect of making a large loss. The booth kept us busy and justified our own feelings of dedication to the principles of library service, although it ultimately confirmed our convictions about the treatment we could expect to receive in the future if we stayed in Roswell.

After clearing out the booth at the end of the week we sat down for another serious talk in front of the fireplace in the house we now feared we would lose. June had been happy about the new friends the library had made through the booth, but she was beginning to see the seriousness of the other matters. I said "The library might be better off if I wasn't here — at least people wouldn't take these irrational swipes at their own institution out of hatred for me."

"Don't be silly — they'd be better off having you even if they had no money and no books," June said, "and the library people know it."

"Thanks," I said. "But did you notice something — I can't trust even your opinion!" I laughed. "Even you are prejudiced!"

When I wanted to relax and think I took long walks over the nearby golf course. Sometimes I would walk in the late evening. I had come to know the place so well that I could walk some distance even in the dark.

The area was very beautiful, with cottonwoods lining the edge of the dry riverbed which cut across the course and the whole town, and an occasional evergreen which the landscape gardeners had planted. Our dog Shandy loved these walks, and on many an occasion we would find a half dozen other dogs trailing after us, just for fun — they had become used to our jaunts.

The dogs in Roswell had become another concern of ours. Most of those accompanying us on our walks were pets belonging to neighbors nearby, but every now and again there would be a stray who would have nowhere to go. Often the strays would follow the riverbed out of town, and as ours was the last house before the open range ours was the house they would stop at. Or perhaps they did sense that they would be cared for.

Most had been owned by military personnel at the air base who abandoned them when they left town. We grew very attached to a great many of them (much to the annoyance of Shandy), and our acquaintances grew tired of our constant inquiry "How would you like to own a nice dog?" We finally found a nice veterinarian who began to take most of them off our hands. He was able to place some of them in good homes, but a few had to be put to sleep. We paid for that.

The dogs somehow symbolized the place for us — it was a town where the innocent got hurt — a beautiful place which really didn't offer the refuge the vista promised. June had visited the city pound and found it a veritable concentration camp for animals. The cats were locked in a dark, unventilated closet and the dogs were kept outside in a tiny cage of chickenwire, exposed to the sun. Those in charge said they had no money to do anything better. They, like the library, were financed by the city council.

We were becoming depressed. More rumors were circulating, one of them being in regard to my supposed drinking habits. I said to June that the last rumor looked like being a self-fulfilling one, as drinking might be the only way to ignore the bastards who were trying to trample us into the ground.

We talked again about the future. "Why don't you resign again, dear?" June said. It sounded like some old, timeworn line from a play, but it was a line I hadn't really listened to. All of a sudden it started to make sense.

As I allowed an uncertain "Yes" to spring to my lips a sense of relief filled me. "Why don't we?" I asked, smiling. Suddenly I felt that the dark closet door had been unlocked, the chickenwire pen had been burst open, and we were free, running down the empty river bed towards the open range — it didn't matter that we might find no comfort there. June felt it too.

I sat down and wrote an OPEN LETTER TO THE PEOPLE OF ROSWELL:

"Have you heard about McShean, the head librarian at the public library, how he has taken some of the books on the Southwest and others he doesn't approve of and hidden them, and won't tell anyone where they are?"

"Have you heard how he's got articles on the sex lives of priests posted — even in the children's department? And how he's been drunk on the job and took six weeks vacation, and brought a load of Buddhist books in? And how he's been spreading sex across the town all this past year with his readings — his morals are non-existent — and what can you suppose about his wife's? And did you hear he himself confessed that the material he was going to read was too rank for children to hear . . . ?"

I freely give back these gems to you, the "good" people of Roswell, to use again on the next public servant you don't like — their use will be as valid against anyone you may choose as against me, for there is not a grain of truth in any of them. But they are circulating . . . circulating better than some of the "trashy" books I have in the library.

This is only a small portion of the lies my wife and I have heard about ourselves since we scheduled the notorious "hippie" poetry reading.

We can take the uninformed criticisms of a man like Truman Pierce, who complained to the County School Board that I'd been withdrawing outdated books, apparently not realizing that this is one of the tasks a librarian is trained and required to do.

We can even face the expressed prejudices of city officials against my beard, my citizenship and my religion (all of which I believe are my own business), knowing that, even when I don't get to answer, the accusations are ridiculous enough to need no answer. But these — Roswell — is this how you keep your town good? How can you go on such an evil campaign of defamation to destroy someone who reads poetry you didn't like?

When we first began hearing some of these things from friends, we discounted them, as we did the anonymous phone calls. People told us this was typical "small town," and we tried to believe them. But we have now cataloged more than twenty slanders — some of them by "responsible" people of this town which are just short of being matters for legal action. Oh, they are clever.
We can't believe this is typical "small town." We have more faith in America than to believe that.

And we don't believe it is all of Roswell that is doing all of this to us. We have many friends here. But few of them wrote to the board of trustees in support of keeping the library open for varied programs, controversial or not . . . and I haven't once heard of any of them reacting violently against the bearers of these slanders, or of trying to impeach an official who discredited us wrongly.

We like our friends here. We even like Roswell, seeing what it could be if it wasn't for the apathy of the truly good people and the viciousness of the self-professed good people.

But we are leaving. I am asking the board to accept my resignation this time as a simple request to be relieved of duty. I will stay the accustomed thirty days to "wrap things up," and will try to sell my house. But we are not "running out on the fight" — there is no fight left to fight.

The struggle was to establish the library as a dynamic center for information and learning. We have seen that there aren't enough people in Roswell who want this enough to fight for it, and that there are people in this town who would destroy us rather than see it happen. My continued presence here would do nothing to further the cause the board and I set out originally to achieve.

Nor am I letting "THEM" run me out. They know, and I know, that I have a right to stay here, alien or no. I am a stubborn Scot, and you can believe I'd stay here 'til doomsday if I thought it would help, but Roswell . . . I think (I hope) I've outgrown you.

Did you know a sermon had been preached about me in town? And that one of the untruths listed above was contained in a letter from a church group to our board of trustees?

I hope that some Christian leaders will recognize the poison within the town and forget their hysterical fear of influences from outside of town — conveyed in poetry. Will there be sermons against slander and scandal mongering? Perhaps as a heathen I have too much faith in Christianity in expecting that.

As for the poetry which was promised to another seventy to one hundred Roswell people — I'm not going to do it. Come and hear me read in Amarillo, or El Paso, or Santa Fe — all places which have requested a program since I did my reading here. Why should I expose myself and my wife to more viciousness? You people who are interested in tuning in the twentieth century had better be prepared to be like us — refugees to some other town in America which understands what freedom and decency are. There I'll read poetry.

No, Roswell. I'd be happy to reason and debate in any struggle on the principles of intellectual freedom and human rights — but when you fight this dirty, I step out of the ring.

Sincerely,

Gordon McShean, Head Librarian.

After I had finished the letter I typed out a short and formal letter of resignation addressed to the board of trustees. Then I called the president of the board and asked if I could talk to him. My resolve was weakening again, and his cordial response on the phone didn't help me.

When I got to his office he said "I'm glad you came, Gordon, because I have something important to talk about to you."

I sat down and smiled politely to show that I was listening.

"I was sorry that I missed all the commotion over the poetry while I was on vacation," he said, "but that appears to have blown over now. I'll see what I can do to smooth over any other matters remaining. That is what I wanted to talk to you about. I have this complaint — " he looked down at his desk as if there was a signed affidavit there (there was nothing). "It seems this lady has a teenage son who has run off to San Francisco to be a hippie. She doesn't know you, and you apparently don't know the son, but she claims that the son ran off to San Francisco because he read about you in our newspaper, with your reading of the poetry — "

I felt the blood rushing to my head as I listened to him. "You can't be serious — you aren't considering this as a valid complaint — you don't think — " I didn't know what to say.

He was most composed, looking down at his desk again. "We have to investigate every and all complaints — "

"Then let me tell you why I came up here to talk to you," I said. "I came here to discuss whether I should resign again or not."

He looked startled.

"Now I am sure I ought to resign — if the board can find nothing better to do than investigate this kind of foolishness, then I have better things to do."

"But you can't resign," he said. "I'll see that the board won't accept your resignation. Let's talk this thing over — "

"I've done more talking than I want to do," I said. "If the board doesn't accept my resignation they will look a little foolish when I leave town anyway. I'll leave in thirty days time. There will be no more bargains with the board — this is a simple resignation, I'm not asking you to fight the mayor for me this time. I hope there will be no recriminations. I appreciate what most of the board members have tried to do for me and the library."

"I'm sorry it has to be like this, Gordon." he said.

"I'm sorry too."

I turned as I was about to leave. "I have this nasty letter to the people of Roswell that I was going to discuss with you. I didn't think it should be printed — but now I think it should. I will take copies to the media, and leave you a copy."

I walked into the street with mixed feelings. I stopped at Walter Geise's bookshop and told him I was leaving.

"Again?" he asked.

"For good," I said. "Repeat — good."

17

Letters

After my letter to the people of Roswell was published, our mailbox and the "letter to the editor" column of the newspaper were crowded with responses. This one touched us:

HAS TO BE SAID

I am only a senior at Goddard High School; I am not one of the leaders of the community, so I don't know whether or not you will listen to what I have to say, but it is something that has to be said.

In the Friday edition of the *Roswell Daily Record* I read an open letter to the public from Mr. Gordon McShean. I hadn't realised how bad the situation had become since the "hippie" poetry reading. My mother works at the library, and even she received some anonymous phone calls, but I assumed they were only pranks. After reading the letter to the people, I found myself embarrassed that I was a citizen of Roswell.

We had a man in charge of the library, and some people want him out of Roswell because he had the intelligence to broaden our horizons. I am not advocating the hippies, but we must accept that they are part of the population. I don't know if they write good poetry or not, but shouldn't we read it before we condemn it?

In my opinion, the cheapest thing anyone can do is spread lies about someone because he disagrees with your ideas. I thought when you grew up you learned to discuss things as adults, but I guess there are no such things as adults, only grown-up children.

I hope someone does something to change my mind about Roswell, because as it is I don't think I'll ever come back after I go to college.

Sarah Cleghorn

A notice appeared in the newspaper after a number of letters on the subject had appeared:

LIBRARY DEBATE
DEADLINE SET

If you want to sound off about our library situation in Public Forum, please do it soon and put your letter into the mail by Thursday night.

Since the issue has been fully debated, the *Record* believes it is time to call a halt. Letters received after Friday morning will be discarded.

Another touching letter was printed the next day. We kept being surprised that people had noticed some of the good things we had tried to do. But now it was too late.

GOOD LIBRARIAN

I'm not at all sure that folk ought to be informed as to what happened to the books that Mr. McShean discarded. However, people of Roswell ought to know how a good librarian thinks when he does do his job and discards some books that have been used and used again and for some time have not been called for. Mr. McShean did not sell the books for so much per pound to a paper dealer as he might have done. He did not send them to the garbage dump as he had the authority to do.

Instead he called the Christian Center because he knew that the Center had a bit of a neighborhood library. Could the Center use some books? If it couldn't others could. I went down and met and talked with a man who knows and loves books. Mr. McShean said to me "Use them in the Center Library. Give them away to children who may read them." I took the books.

Some of them are in the Christian Center now. Some of them are in other Centers where people come who haven't the transportation nor perhaps the energy to walk downtown to the library. But some of the books will be read. Books are to be used and even in discarding some from the overcrowded shelves of the public library Mr. McShean — in his understanding that books are to be distributed where they can best be read — gave them away to people. There seem to be those who would keep books on shelves and discard people.

Sincerely,
(Reverend) R.Q. Adams

June was moved to write something very heartfelt. We anticipated that the debate would be over soon and that we should say something which would remove the attention from ourselves to the real casualty of the affair, Roswell.

Dear Editor:

Many people have shown their sincere sympathy and willingness to help us. We are thankful for this, but have made up our minds to leave Roswell. Neither Gordon nor I have been able to relax since the "hippie" controversy started.

There is nothing anyone can do for us; Roswell needs the help!

There are still some people in town who want to help Roswell. Help them.

This is what you can do for Roswell. A town is only a town if you make it your town.

Sincerely,

June McShean

We had thought that things would quiet down now that we were leaving. The newspaper had said the debate was over. People were starting to say goodbye. But the last word was still to be said. The letters continued to pour in, and the newspaper ignored the deadline it had set. There were people who were anxious to rekindle our love for the town before we left — and there were people who hoped to destroy us.

Here are only a few from the dozens that were written:

To the Editor:

I have lived in Roswell just three and a half years and find that it is a nice place to live and find that people are very friendly. We have had visitors from out of state to give complimentary remarks regarding the friendliness of the people here, even including the police department.

The reason I am writing this letter to you is that I want to get my two cents' worth in regarding the hippie poetry reading in Roswell Public Library.

First of all, I want the people that are in charge of the library to know that I didn't make any phone calls nor did I tell any lies about them. I am neither a Baptist nor a John Bircher but I am a Christian.

Second, I feel we all should turn to the Word of God to know the truth. In Acts 19: 19 and 20 people that gave their hearts to Christ did the following: "Many of them also which used curious arts brought their books together, and burned them before all men: and they counted the price of them, and found it fifty thousand pieces of silver. So mightily grew the Word of God."

Paul writes to the Corinthian Church in Corinthians 1: 18-25, "For the preaching of the cross is to them that perish foolishness; but unto us which are saved it is the power of God. For it is written, I will destroy the wisdom of the wise, and will bring to nothing the understanding of the prudent. Where is the wise? where is the scribe? where is the disputer of this world? Hath not God made foolish the wisdom of this world?"

"For after that in the wisdom of God the world by wisdom knew not God, it pleased God by the foolishness of preaching to save them that believe. For the Jews require the sign and the Greeks seek after wisdom: But we preach Christ crucified, unto the Jews a stumbling block, and unto the Greeks foolishness; But unto them which are called, both Jews and Greeks, Christ the power of God, and the wisdom of God. Because the foolishness of God is wiser than men; and the weakness of God is stronger than men." The person that takes a public office and tries to reform the public culture has to accept the repercussions that will come from such a change. Christ came to change the religious realm with truth and he ended up standing alone and being crucified. Yet today his message is real life to those that will accept and keep it.

Third, I have no apology to make for those that made the anonymous phone calls, preached rumors from the pulpit or told lies to others. I don't see where hippie poetry could do much good to help humanity to solve their problems or to live a good life, when these hippies kill, they rape, and they give each others pills to destroy their minds. Yes, we have all sinned and come short of the kingdom of God but Jesus said that unless we "repent, ye shall all likewise perish" in Luke 13: 3. I John 1: 9 tells us "If we confess our sins, He is faithful and just to forgive us our sins, and to cleanse us from all unrighteousness."

May God help us all build a better community spiritual and education wise for the glory of God and the future of our children.

Yours for a better community,
Willard W. Metz

To the Public Forum:

Yes! They have done it. They have lost the most progressive Head Librarian this town has ever had. They lost him by being provincial and hickish. He was in tune with the modern and the future, but he was out of tune with the nearsighted. So the nearsighted drove him away.

A few months ago he was offered employment in a distant city at nearly twice his salary here, but he turned it down because he felt he had a mission to bring our library up to date. These good intentions are now dead, and we will settle back into the stagnant water from which we were so nearly lifted.

The soft voice of Gordon McShean will be heard again in other towns. It will be for their good. We are the loser.

I, personally, am partially to blame. I did not stand up and speak out. Let us learn from this, and always be ready to make a stand when someone trying to help us needs support.

Fearl M. Parker

Dear Mr. Editor:

Some of our readers and writers are getting involved in their thinking and talking about libraries and academic freedom and climate of hate and all that kind of talk. The whole thing is really kind of easy to figure.

Things are right or they are wrong — as simple as that. Even our Lord said those who were not for Him were against Him. People know there are hippies who have been given far too much publicity but libraries are places to store knowledge. Librarians are there to help people find it. If folks are going to get two views and always the same two views to every question rather than two opposing views then there is no so-called academic freedom. And, to discuss these academic matters someone has to be a member of *la academe* as the French call it.

Adults can take all kinds of views and viewpoints but the kids may not be ready for it. Is it right or is it wrong? If someone wanted to have a dance in a church would that be academic freedom or just license to blaspheme? Why not have filthy picture shows in the library? You could get a big audience and more friends. When a fellow comes to a new place he should not try to change anything to suit himself so fast but make a few adjustments himself. Freedom for professors to march with agitators is also academic freedom but is not right. This phrase is down at the heels. Is it good or evil? Brotherhood and religion not involved in such a question, as readers write about.

Yours truly,
John Petrakis

The former librarian wrote:

Editor:

I question your editorial policy in closing Public Forum debate on an issue vital to the civic and cultural growth of Roswell.

Is a newspaper fair to its public when it cuts off discussion of a controversy that was aggravated and embittered by its own sensational news reporting?

Because people were poorly informed, many have spoken unwisely and intemperately, and without time for reflection. Second thoughts are best. Why not give our responsible, sound-thinking citizens a chance to express themselves after full consideration of the damage done our library and our community by the disgraceful happenings of the past few weeks?

Betty Nicholas

Quite a few more letters were to be seen before the matter would be over. Finally there was this:

Letter to the editor:

During the past week nearly one hundred citizens of Roswell have joined this irate housewife in signing the following statement:

"We, the undersigned . . . do hereby affirm and petition that Gordon McShean, head librarian of the Roswell Public Library, has administered his duties and the policies of the Library Board of Trustees in a manner deserving of gratitude and admiration; that the Board of Trustees is to be commended for establishing a Statement of Policy and incorporating therein the Library Bill of Rights and the Freedom to Read Statement and holding firm to this policy under pressure.

"That the Mayor and City Council inform themselves concerning the function and policy of the library, and that they call on the Board of Trustees to conduct a public hearing on any future controversy so that the facts may be presented and public scandal avoided.

"We renounce the shameful treatment afforded our librarian and the lack of respect shown our library board of trustees, and we hope that the board can promptly obtain the services of another Master of Library Science to continue the policies and the vigorous programs initiated by Mr. McShean."

> Anyone wishing to add their
> names to this petition may con-
> tact me . . . we plan to for-
> ward same to the parties in-
> volved, as well as to the New
> Mexico Library Association.
> Sincerely,
> Mrs. Robert N. Enfield

It was a nice going away present for us. We had been unable to sell our house and were faced with the prospect of making a loss to the mortgage company. We sold some of our furniture at auction and got peanuts for it. We needed cheering up.

I went to rent a trailer to load our personal belongings. One of the city councilmen owned the franchise for rental trailers. The deal he made me was reasonable enough. I guessed he was of the opinion that it was the most pleasant piece of business he'd done in a while.

The day we chose to leave Roswell was quiet. There had been six vultures perched on the branches of trees close to the foot of our garden in the previous days — it sounds like fiction, but the newspaper even made note of the circumstance — and now they were gone.

We took a last look around the house and garden. We didn't know if the new trees I had planted would survive. Some weeks previously we had received a threatening telephone call which had included a threat to burn a cross on our front lawn. My response had been "If there is a cross burned on my lawn, another will burn there each night for a month, I promise!" I had been embittered because in Scotland the burning cross is traditionally the sign to rally one's neighbors for aid when an attack is threatened from outside. My threat to keep a cross burning may have been enough to discourage those who wished to intimidate me. The lawn was unsullied.

I had prepared a marker for our lawn. We had found a weatherbeaten board which had reminded us of a tombstone in the traditional Western "boot hill" cemeteries. I had spent some time carving the legend

> here rested
> in peace
> THE MC SHEANS
> 1966-67.

Now I planted this in the middle of the lawn, and placed a plastic flower in a coke bottle in front of it. It gave us the courage to smile as we drove away. But we needn't have worried about putting up a front — we didn't see anyone we knew as we drove to the edge of town.

We were only a few miles out of town when one of our tires blew out, and we had to spend hours on the road waiting for a spare to be brought (our own spare was buried under all the stuff we had packed). We traveled ninety miles that day. June had developed a severe stomach ailment by the time we got going again, and we were both miserable.

I've often said to June since, that Roswell would be a nice place to go if one had independent means. You could say "To hell with all the old fogies!" and go your own way. There'd be a lot of people who would appreciate a free man.

"Independent means!" June laughs. "It would be nice just to have a regular paycheck again!"

Since then Roswell has lost even more of its population, stores stand empty, and some streets have hardly one home occupied. One of our friends committed suicide. The superintendent of schools was forced to leave, and the symphony conductor, the curator of the museum and our television announcer friend all chose to move elsewhere. The Book Mine closed and Walter and his wife vanished, letters being returned "addressee unknown." It is all very sad. We never did hear if the play I was supposed to direct was ever presented. We don't know if the little theatre group still performs. Maybe there are still a few people there hanging on to "culture." We hope so.

We had one final satisfaction, some months later, when we opened a copy of *Library Journal* and saw that THE UGLY AMERICAN AWARD OF THE YEAR had been awarded to the Mayor of Roswell by the magazine. He was quoted as having said about me "He's not an American citizen and he wears that beard. And he's a Buddhist. If you understand that, you understand the type of person he is."

I was still trying to discover what kind of person I was — but I had the satisfaction of knowing that half the librarians in the U.S. knew what kind of man the mayor was. I wondered if the mayor liked himself.

18

Retribution

Everything I had done in Roswell was in accordance with professional library principles. Librarians get very misty-eyed when discussing these progressive principles at conferences — discussion threatens no one. We were soon to discover that a lot of complaisant people who were dedicated to the library as a quiet temple for the cultivation of civic niceties felt threatened by us.

I had long known that some librarians' censorship consciousness was little more than dogma-mumbling. The idea of a library freed from the prejudices of their "liberal" intellects was beyond most of them. Their failure to offer me more than paper support when I was down to the crunch confirmed this. But I was unprepared for the retribution which was to follow — and which these realizations might have foretold.

I found that I had been almost totally shut out of the profession. Even though I was still publicly a "nice guy" who had stood up for a professional principle, the fine job offers and the opportunities for advanced study which had been showered on me when I was simply a nice "innovative" young librarian were no longer available. There was no job

shortage in the profession then — the libraries were crying
out for more people with professional qualifications — but I
found that in the next two years the best I could do was
take a short-term job in rural Iowa, then attempt to fill my
enforced idleness by writing and taking a few more courses
at the university. June found jobs where she could to keep
us going. It was cruel.

In our eyes our predicament made hypocrisy seem to be
the major characteristic of my profession. We felt we had
nothing to apologize for, and yet the entire library field
seemed to be telling us that we were well-intentioned misfits
which they could as well do without. I submitted more than
a hundred applications to libraries, and began to feel privi-
leged if I received a form letter in acknowledgment. Many
did not even bother to respond. The situation brought that
old question back to my lips: had I been right in choosing
librarianship as a career?

As these depressing thoughts and circumstances impressed themselves upon us we had a surprising revelation.
I had previously considered that my struggles against the
censors — and my hope of making an "honest woman" out
of the library profession — had been born of an aery view
of library service which was held by only myself and a few
other "nuts" (I had descended to the point of calling myself
names). But as I traveled from job interview to library conference to job interview from one end of the country to the
other (I even had applications on file in a number of libraries
abroad) I kept bumping into librarians here and there who
were glad to tell me they knew me. I found that there were
solitary librarians who had been following what I had been
doing in Roswell and who had somehow idealized me.

I'm sure it came as a disappointment to some of them
to find out that I was human — depressingly and vulnerably
human at this point — but their high opinion of what I had

done gave me the courage I needed to continue. It was comforting to know that there were others who shared my convictions. It meant that there might still be hope for the profession and for my future in it, if I could just find the right people and a community which realized its need for the kind of service we could offer.

It has been said that my experience in Roswell appeared to be one of the first of a wave of repressive actions taken against librarians. But things were simply continuing as they had for years. The only change was that my own persecution had been over an issue so patently silly that it had gained national attention and sympathy. This had spurred others to report more fully what had been happening to them.

People had stood their ground and tried to gain professional support at other times. Perhaps their opposition had been more credible and their stand less newsworthy. Except among people close to the victims, the failure of the profession to act had attracted little attention. The machinery of the associations had been designed for good public relations. Now there had been a call for help that the public expected to see answered; the machinery had tried to change into non-existent gears; the grinding sounds from the professional organizations were deafening.

The silly people of Roswell — who wanted their poets dead or not at all — had been responsible for triggering a reaction in libraries which was felt across the nation. Librarians, even if only a few idealistic ones, were finding the strength to resist the censors, and they were pressuring their associations to deliver on their promises.

It was good to find kindred spirits in the profession. But I was unhappy to discover that such people were under attack all across the nation. The censors sometimes discovered these "spirits" before we did, and moved to label them "evil." They didn't always know if they had a fighter on their hands, however, and this gave us some breathing space before censorship situations escalated. We were learning how to prepare for them.

We knew if a fighter had been challenged when the calls for help came through. There was no prevarication. Principled people will stand in front of a road-roller if necessary. We frequently found ourselves anticipating the necessity of having to resuscitate a flattened fellow-in-freedom.

Many cases of attempts to censor libraries were reported in the next two years (and unfortunately the reports continue to come in, along with reports of efforts to intimidate the press). Michigan, California, Virginia, New Jersey, Washington, New York, Missouri and numerous other places spring to mind. We heard about them if there was open resistance or abject surrender. Who can doubt that every state in the union would have been represented twice over if all of the deals and compromises had been reported?

The *Newsletter on Intellectual Freedom* devised a reporting method which showed its subscribers (mostly members of the American Library Association) the "hot spots" for censorship in the nation by placing stars on a map of the U.S. There was hardly a month when America could not claim to be a star-spangled nation.

I wish I could say that the librarians who now found themselves in trouble faced a more promising future. Some had families to support. Some became involved in legal battles which drained their resources. Some became ill under the strain of the insults, lies and threats they had to face. At least one suffered all of these misfortunes. The majority found themselves without jobs — at least — and had a difficult time finding other positions.

There were cases of physical assaults being made upon librarians and death threats being received. The courage shown by some librarians in the face of this kind of intimidation was nothing short of amazing. Martyrdom for the cause offered no rewards beyond the satisfaction of having stood for a principle, identification with a band of impoverished veteran censorship fighters, and a certain amount of personal notoriety.

It was ironic that when the professional associations deigned to honor persons who had contributed to the struggle against the censors it was often those who had been notable for their theoretical and philosophical contributions to the professional literature who were chosen; the people who had struggled with the realities of censorship were somehow passed over.

Our jolly band of censorship fighters did help to accomplish a few things that would be of some help to those finding themselves under attack in the future. Funds were established to aid librarians who might be in distress because of censorship controversies. Investigatory procedures and even certain punitive measures were authorized by the American Library Association to back up their anti-censorship statements. Local intellectual freedom committees still tended to be overawed and timid when faced with crises, but they were more aware of the demand for action. These changes were heartening to some, but have been slight comfort for the censorship victims and the libertarians — censorship grows apace.

It will take the assistance of the public to change things. Librarians can show the way, but that is all. A few ridiculous people can promote a panic. A few caring people could demand a proper library in their community to serve the needs of overyone.

The library profession has been comforted for many years by the knowledge that political extremists, comic book addicts, film buffs, pornography readers, video freaks, members of minority races and rock-music hounds were unlikely to band together to demand their rightful share of the library's purchasing dollar. It has been too easy for the profession to pay lip service to the ideal of service for all — and quietly to suppress those librarians who did not go along with the conspiracy.

It is little wonder that the dissenters in the library profession disassociated themselves from the old image of the librarian. If social responsibility was ridiculous, then they would be ridiculous. Serious expressions of concern had been disregarded. They began to emulate the life styles and expressions of the hippie and yippie groups. They may well have appeared ridiculous.

The situation did not improve when they then attempted to communicate with their placid and straight — and employed — colleagues. The generation gap — which in this case had little to do with age, since many of the "new" people were at least middle aged — had invaded the profession. Librarians perhaps didn't need the new culture. But the new culture needed librarians. All we had to do was convince the new culture of that, and keep from starving.

19

Bellybuttons

I was attending a conference of young, radical librarians in a large city on the Eastern seaboard of the United States. I have to admit, however, that some of us did not quite measure up to that nomenclature. I had traveled a considerable distance in the most economical ways that I could find, and I was feeling old and pooped. We had had a few meetings already, and there were still more to be held. Some would sit late into the night "rapping." All I had to look forward to was a sleeping bag on the floor of a sympathetic colleague's kitchen.

We had discussed such things as "Should librarians have a code of professional ethics?" and "Should a responsible librarian join the American Library Association?" The subjects we had chosen made us feel quite important.

The meetings had positively demonstrated that none of us had any respect for censorship or the withholding of information in whatever form it might take — some of us didn't even know when to shut up. But I consoled myself with the knowledge that hot air is just as much a feature of the more traditional professional meetings.

There was more heat in our radical utterances, which

may account for the fact that our hot air had a different effect from the hot air at the usual meetings where one had a difficult time staying awake; at our meetings you couldn't doze off even if you wanted to.

The listener was constantly made aware that this was the rhetoric which was capable of striking terror into the hearts of the old traditional type of conference officer. The expression "Point of order, Mr. Chairman!" had been replaced by an unabashed "Bullshit!" The old "Hear, hear!" which had once signified wholehearted agreement under the rules of Mr. Roberts had been replaced by "Right on!"

These were the new conceits which were causing the old-style officers to imagine themselves being forcibly thrown from the podium by some wild feminist, gay liberationist or what-have-you in some anarchist bid for power. One could hardly blame the kids for using them — they were undeniably effective.

Had these people known of the insecurity which motivated the rantings of some of these "radicals," and had they known of the violent clashes of opinion which occurred even in a gathering such as this — dedicated to solidarity — they would never have lost another wink of sleep.

Most of us who were participants can take some of the blame for the ranting and raving. Forcefulness had become a style of presentation, an assurance of strongly held ideals, an expression of offended dignity and an assertion of honesty. It was effective in startling the more inhibited meeting-goer into paying attention. But when you had a roomful of activists all schooled in the same techniques (and I include myself) — each espousing a different cause and seeing those who differed from them as *the enemy* — it could get to be a prodigious pain in the posterior.

I had attended the conference in order to participate in the establishment of a fund to assist librarians who had been fired for fighting censors. I had fortunately been able to survive without such assistance myself, but I wanted to make sure that there were funds available for those who might not be so lucky in the future. I was gratified to be able to participate in the successful establishment of the fund shortly after my arrival (becoming one of the directors of the National Freedom Fund for Librarians). Now I was able to participate in the other meetings at my leisure.

I found that some of the meetings were being used as platforms for ego-centered activities more likely to provoke negative reactions in the audience than to accomplish anything constructive.

There were still some good causes represented. Those interested in discrimination in library hiring made some good points — "ethnic minorities" were not getting the training and education to allow them to take jobs which might be open to them, and they suffered the same fate as women when they did get a job, seldom being able to participate in administration.

But there was always the person ready to destroy the receptiveness of the audience to indulge his or her own biases. There was the feminist who accused all men of being chauvinist, and the black who accused all non-blacks of being racist. It was blatant reverse discrimination — perhaps justified by the viciousness of the discrimination they suffered. Their charges were self-defeating and would be useful only as elements of a mass suicide pact. If their assertions were true there was no point in our being there or attempting to talk to one another, for change was impossible. But there was no use in pointing this out.

There were other expressions of disharmony — personal attacks on those who disagreed, accusations of collusion with the establishment — it was all stuff we'd heard so many times before, stuff which has plagued every liberal, hip, radical, socialist (maybe even John Birch Society) meeting, games we should have been tired of. I was tired.

I was just getting ready to leave in disgust when I heard giggling coming from a room further down the hotel corridor. It offered a welcome diversion to investigate the source. I invariably feel some kind of guilt for disapproving of a whole roomful of people at once — "what kind of elitist intellectual am I becoming?" I ask myself. Now I could pretend to myself that I had a legitimate reason to leave.

As I went out into the corridor I started to pass two other librarians who had remained outside, apparently persons also feeling the futility of the meetings. "Are they still bitching in there?" one of them asked me. I nodded. "It's goddamn ridiculous — they never get anything done except pass airy-fairy resolutions about brotherhood and service to the people," the corridor inhabitant said. I nodded dumbly. She was determined to continue her condemnation. "They never do anything to change the system," she said. "Goddamn, they make me sick!"

The criticism seemed hardly more constructive than the comments being made in the room I had just left. The giggles from the room further down the hall were getting louder, and proving infectious — to me at least.

"It sounds like some people have found some non-destructive activities," I said, nodding in the direction of the sounds. "What's going on in there?"

"They are worse," my sourfaced colleague snapped. "They were supposed to have an information meeting or something or other, and when nobody showed up they got drinks and started playing around. You'd think they could find something better to do."

"Like the people in there?" I asked, pointing to the room I had just left. I allowed a smirk to appear on my face. "Ever hear of the cliche, 'If you can't say something nice, don't say anything at all?'" As I walked down the corridor to the giggling meeting I could hear displeased snorts from the two I had left standing in the corridor.

The giggling in the other room grew in volume as the audience was increased by my presence. On the floor lay a red-faced male librarian, pinioned by a number of healthy young female librarians. The girls were doing the giggling, while he was grunting and wriggling and swearing under his breath. Their limbs were thrashing this way and that (I took special note of the untrousered ones), and it really was difficult to tell which portion of anatomy belonged to whom. Above them a staid-looking middle aged lady stood holding a paper cup poised in the air.

"Get his shirt up, get his shirt up!" one of the young women giggled.

I couldn't help laughing. "What the hell are you doing?" I asked. "Is this a men-against-women thing? You need help, old buddy?"

"We only want to see if he has an inner or an outer belly button," one of the girls in the heap said, still giggling as she spoke. With that she made a concerted effort and managed to pull the man's clothing up so that his navel was exposed. It was definitely an inverted umbilicus which was discovered. There was an "ohh" from some of the girls.

"Too bad — " one of the girls said. "We'll find an outer belly button yet. *Hold* him!" she yelled as the man started to struggle again to release himself.

"What'll you do if you find one?" I asked.

"— Don't know, just curious!" They grabbed his hands and feet more firmly. "Hold him tight" "Here it comes! Now!" one of them said.

Suddenly the purpose of the lady with the paper cup became clear. The man bucked and hollered as ice water from the cupful of ice cubes was slowly dripped upon his midriff, dropping down to form a pool in his sunken belly button.

"Goddamn sadists!" the man yelled, but he was half laughing all the time. I watched as they continued the treatment. The skin where the ice water dripped began to turn red. "I'm going to get frostbite on my belly!" he said.

"It'll be better than getting your ass frozen off," one of the younger and more innocent looking ladies said.

"Yeh, you won't have a beer belly any more," another quipped.

"Running out of ice," the dripper said.

I was still standing watching, feeling my spirits lift. "What would you do with the ice if you came across someone with an outer belly button?" I asked. "Then the icewater wouldn't form a pool."

"We'll cross that bridge when we come to it," the lady with the icewater said. "We might just slip it down his pants." Then she turned to look at me with renewed interest. "Say, what kind of belly button do you have?" She looked at the other girls and then back at me as I retreated towards the door. "Do you think he's got an inner or an outer?"

As I raced down the hotel corridor the girls were still extricating themselves from the tangle their limbs had made. "We'll get you later!" they yelled.

"Ohhh, *that's* better," I heard the man say as they released him.

I walked out into the street searching for a hotdog stand — suddenly having developed an appetite — and smiling as I thought of the scene I had just left.

There was hope for librarians if they could just discuss serious issues and keep their sense of humor. The two groups in the different rooms on the same hotel corridor were made up of the same kind of people. Sooner or later they would have to come together. People with inner and outer belly buttons were getting jobs in libraries without discrimination. It was a start. Now a hotdog and a cosy sleeping bag would make the whole trip seem worthwhile. Someday there might even be a job for a blue-eyed librarian like me.

20

California

In California I began to realize the universality of the censorship problem. We had returned to California (it was my wife's home state and we had lived there prior to going to New Mexico), where I continued to look for library work while earning a living whatever way I could. Libraries were not yet ready for me. I wrote articles for magazines. I found I had plenty of time to explore the dimensions of censorship.

I had visited almost every library the length and breadth of California when I happened to stop at Richmond, in the San Francisco Bay area, to ask if there might be work. "Gordon!" the librarian exclaimed, "I'd hoped to meet you — I've read about what you have done, and I'm a great admirer of yours!" I rapidly had to discard my diffident job-hunting mien as I was confronted with this instant friendship. His welcome was sorely needed, for I had been put off by so many of the people I had met on my rounds, and had wasted more hours filling out application forms for jobs which never materialized that I was beginning to be sorely discouraged. I did not care if he had a job for me or not — the smiling welcome was what I needed.

The librarian's name was John Forsman, and he had built himself a reputation as an innovative young librarian too. His library was attracting new people, his film programs were causing favorable comment, and he was known as a dynamic and friendly administrator. It was perhaps easy to predict what he would subsequently tell me.

Over a friendly cup of coffee, and after meeting various of his staff members and exchanging pleasantries, he said to me quietly, "You can't know how pleased I am to see you — I am facing an attack by the censors here too — I'd appreciate whatever help and advice you can give me."

I learned that in the few weeks prior to my arrival he had started to receive reports of a campaign building against him and the library's policy on collecting books and magazines. Complaints were based upon the local "underground" newspaper the *Berkeley Barb* (Richmond and Berkeley adjoin one another) and the magazine *Avant Garde*, an arty, glossy periodical which had national distribution. The *Los Angeles Free Press*, another "underground" newspaper, was also mentioned.

The pressure had first been felt in a library some miles from Richmond. There the same items were complained about and the librarian quietly capitulated by putting them on shelves which were difficult to find — the act was nothing but censorship, even if no one could say the librarian removed them from the collection. It was a discreditable thing to do, we both agreed. "I'll see the censors in hell before I hide anything in my library," John said to me.

"How can I help?" I asked. "I'd like to be one of the notorious troublemakers who are always being blamed for troubles at home by the politicians — I'd like to be an 'outside agitator'!"

It was the beginning of a good friendship — and a long and weary fight with the censors. I spent many hours in Richmond helping John and his supporters map strategy and avoid pitfalls. The actions of his attackers appeared to be from the same blueprints used in Roswell. The one change was that the state intellectual freedom committee did work closely with John's librarians. The librarians seemed more satisfied that their part in the struggle was proper — John had twice the support that I had, and it came when he needed it. The publicity of Roswell and the precedent it had set were helping a great deal.

But even with the support, John's fight was a difficult one. The terrible part of the conflict, as it had been in my own case, was the circulation of morale-damaging slanders which soon surrounded Forsman and his wife. His staff had a share of the libels too. As usual, there was never anyone who could be pinpointed as the source.

Particular magazines were not really at issue. The censors were attacking the whole run of each periodical, demanding that subscriptions be canceled. They doubtless knew that we would find *prior* censorship — censorship of a publication not yet published — doubly to be condemned. They had simply baited their hook with these titles. They had guaranteed themselves a big fish, as it was predictable that smaller fish would scurry away; they obviously expected the big fish to put up a fight.

The issue was not whether things would stay on the library shelves, but whether a librarian who refused to bend to political pressure would be allowed to continue to work. There are people who have a vested interest in seeing that the important institutions in America conform to their demands. To them the free access to information is not the safeguard of democracy and the right of the individual, as most of us believe, but is instead an invitation to anarchy. Their distrust of the intelligence of the common man is amazing. Their paranoia over the intentions of the intellectuals in society is devastating. And their trust in "big government" to cure the ills of society — but only certain ills — would be funny if it was not so tragic.

They had hooked a fish, and all they had to do now

was land him. Their bait did not have quite so many barbs in it as the name of the newspaper, the *Berkeley Barb* might have suggested. The periodicals were quite tame compared to some "hard core" materials available in liquor stores within walking distance of the library.

The *Barb* had one strident claim to be in any library in the area: it had the best community calendar of educational, recreational and cultural events available. No community-conscious institution could afford to be without it. The fact that it also carried a few articles which might be politically offensive made it a suitable target — those who had been offended were likely to give the attack their support.

Avant Garde was an entirely different kind of publication. Its editor was Ralph Ginzburg. A combination of top-name contributors, a selective advertising campaign, a glossy format and a generous portion of uninhibited artistic expression had made it a much-talked-about publication. There was no doubt of its artistic pretentions or of the massive support it enjoyed among members of the intellectual community. As such, it deserved a place in the library.

The *Los Angeles Free Press* was not seriously in contention — although there was no doubt that it would be banned from the library along with the others if the censors had their way. It was probably the most comprehensive of the underground newspapers of the time. By virtue of its large advertising revenues it was able to cover events across the nation more completely than other "anti-establishment" sources. Although its political view was not stated, it could easily be seen as promoting leftist viewpoints; this was probably as much to blame for it being on the censor's list as any objectionable advertisements in its classified section (where thinly veiled solicitation for sex partners could be found).

The political aspect of the censorship struggle was seldom

mentioned by the censors. The moral question — concerning adults — was also taboo to them. It is probable that they realized they would lose support if they were open about their interest in controlling the political and moral expressions available to adults. There is no question that they did have a strong interest in such control. Their choice of publications and their decision to attack the library instead of the publishers or booksellers testified to their intent.

But their inability to be open about these matters dictated that they instead concentrate upon the supposed dangers which face children exposed to "immoral" writings and illustrations. It did not matter that proof of harm resulting from exposure to such materials has yet to be discovered. The cry, "What will they do to our children?" rang especially loud when the magazine *Avant Garde* was mentioned.

I was occasionally moved, at the meetings I attended, to describe my own juvenile searchings for erotic stimuli. Since I seemed to be the only one who remembered such experiences, or was the only one prepared to be honest about them (I refuse to believe that the experiences were unique), I thought that the confessions might defuse the censor's arguments. After all, hadn't I become a respectable member of the community, a librarian? But I had to remind myself that the political implications would require them to impute immorality to anyone making such testimony.

Avant Garde contained graphic materials which the censors found useful to hold up for their audiences while making denunciations of the artist's intentions to debauch the minds of children. There were many meetings — some limited to people attacking the library and the librarian, some to those who ran to the library's defense, and a few general meetings.

Newspapers and radio and television took note of the controversy — they too found the subject of the seduction of the young to be "good copy." The "letters to the editor" columns of some newspapers carried citizens' comments, although the letter-writing campaign we had experienced in the controversy in New Mexico was not repeated — doubtless because there were newspapers with differing editorial viewpoints.

Mrs. Dorothy Strindberg and Mrs. Royce Klock were the organizers of most of the attacks upon the library. Mrs. Strindberg's testimony at the much celebrated meeting of the Richmond City Council which climaxed the controversy went like this:

> Why I'm speaking this evening and objecting to the *Avant Garde* and the *Berkeley Barb* being in our library is the very fact — the things were mentioned here tonight — the uprise of delinquency, crime, and so forth.
>
> I sit in the council tonight and see all these young boys lined up from our baseball club. I'm sitting with the *Avant Garde!* The *Avant Garde* and the *Berkeley Barb,* I understand, is available to children from seventh and eighth grade. I looked at those boys and I thought "Here's something we all want, and we're going to give it to 'em: a good, clean, healthy sport. We want good, clean living conditions, better conditions . . . . "
>
> I will continue to object of the *Berkeley Barb* and the *Avant* [sic] being in our library. I don't think that it is good to have it there [holding up a copy of *Avant Garde*]. It adds no culture and no dignity to it . . . . If anyone could come up here tonight and explain this picture to me and tell me what this adds to the library — to dignity — what this adds to a education of a child's mind, I as a good sport would be willing to back down. And I would go along if they could prove to me that a seventh or eighth grader should be taught this.
>
> Now as we all know, sex is something we don't hide from or stick our head in the sand — it exists. There's a beautiful side and an ugly side. But should we subject

children to it, that has an immature mind for the ugly side of it — when all we are hollering now is better education, better living conditions, better health conditions? These are unhealthy illustrations [pertaining?] to sex.

[Waving magazine in the air] I object because I don't think my daughter should be seeing it — she goes to the public library. I object because I have four foster children that I'm taking care of and helping to give love and affection and care to.

— I ask, please, don't pollute a child's mind! Pollution of the mind can be a terrible thing! Now I was told by some of our councilmen that this was *good* to expose a child to. Gentlemen, we're not talking about measles, we're talking about somethin's more serious than a child's disease. We're talking about how we're taxed and fight for the mentally ill and the retarded children. Then *why* can't we help to keep the good healthy minds healthy? Why can't we give a kid a break?

And today I say, how can we taxpapers be taxed for retardation, better living conditions, and give people what they are asking for, a good, clean, decent community — what we're being taxed for? Is that such a crime?

If the crime of a physical body — rape — is a crime — then to rape a young child's mind is a crime too. And I'm here to take care of all the children that don't know what's being *forced* upon them! We're violating a child's rights by *forcing* the issue of sex in a perverted manner, an uneducational manner . . . .

I'm only a mother fighting not for my children, but for all the youth in our community. You know when you are on the upgrade, not the downgrade. And I always will tend to build up my community, not tear it down. (Applause)

Mrs. Strindberg's appeal — like the appeal of so many

others bent on controlling the media — could tempt one to presume that there was sincerity in her concern. There probably was — as far as she enunciated her concern. Her attempts to disclaim an interest in restricting publications beyond the protection of children rang hollow, however. The publications would necessarily be denied to all if she and her group had their way.

It is interesting to consider how much the fear of the loss of a child's innocence played in the minds of those censors who were honestly motivated (one can only presume that there must occasionally be a person so obsessed with the subject of child debauching that he or she cannot see beyond that subject to the general effects of prohibitions upon other people). Those of us who remember our childhood well are unlikely to give credence to any suggestion of the existence of such innocence. An honest consultation with one of today's aware young people will rapidly dispel any illusion of the existence of such a condition. The desire of the censors to *create* the condition is not only a denial of the child's rights but a denial of the child's humanity. (Innocence probably exists in only one creature, the rookie librarian, and it lasts only a moment, being dispelled at the first job interview.)

The argument for the children had been made in Roswell against *Playboy* in the same way as it was being made in Richmond against *Avant Garde.* It was like a Santa Claus syndrome, a desperate effort to keep children boxed in to the established mythology, away from reality or the freedom to create original fantasies — and unnaturally dependent upon parental interpretation in coping with ordinary, every-day events. One wondered what it would profit the censors to suppress publications which might inform children that they have genitals and that some people use these organs for purposes other than going to the bathroom. It appeared to be unimportant to these upholders of fiction-as-a-better-way

-of-life that the explanations they offered the exploring mind of a child might do more harm than the truth. The censors themselves had been victims of such behavior. They seemed determined to make humanity suffer for eternity to justify the suffering they had endured. One was sometimes moved to pity by the obvious crippling effects their upbringing had had on them.

But there was little time to indulge in the luxury of pity when the children and society itself were being threatened. There was no possibility of convincing the censors of the error of their ways — all we could do was attempt to stop the damage their efforts might accomplish in distorting our institutions to implement their ends. We could not protest to them that a child is naturally endowed with an enquiring mind and will grasp such ideas as he or she is ready for *and disregard others* — the censor knew the child's mind was pliant, and that made it fair game. The censor was determined to leave his impress, and deny access to all others.

The tyranny of the censorious adult over the child — a tradition of long standing — was being challenged by the new knowledge. The tyrant was attempting to extend the range of its tyranny and neutralize the challenge. If it succeeded we all could become subject to that dictatorship. Is it any wonder that we believed more than children's minds were involved when we heard the rhetoric of the censors?

21

Dog Days

There were some lighter moments too. I was busy writing my first autobiographical book, and had a number of other writing projects going at the same time — magazine articles and a children's book. Our budget was tight (we were living largely off our savings — June had occasional clerical or secretarial jobs from an agency), but we were able to go on camping trips, see a movie now and then, and enjoy long walks along the bay shore near our apartment in Alameda.

Our dog Shandy had plenty of attention. Not only did he enjoy the luxury of having one or another of us home much of the time, he was also blessed by the apartment landlady's rule against pets — we had to pretend that he was my mother's dog and that he was only left with us occasionally. That meant — for credibility — that he had to spend some time at my parents' place in nearby Oakland. Accordingly, he had two homes — and it was opportune to have him at the one where he was likely to get the greatest attention. If it hadn't been for the Richmond censors, who messed up our schedules many times, he would have become thoroughly spoiled.

22

Opinions

My wife and I had attended a number of meetings in homes in the Richmond-Berkeley area to do what we could to support the beleaguered librarians and the library commission in Richmond. These meetings were often unpleasant. Some felt they knew how to stand on principle better than others, and a yelling match sometimes resulted. It was understandable considering the pressure some had to face.

The meetings did let each of us know what the other was doing, and caused some people to assist who might otherwise have let things go. They also helped us to justify our call to the California Library Association for a stand against the censors.

The library commission was being pressured by the city council to give in to censorship — there was a threat to remove part of the commission's responsibility. It seemed probable that certain of its members would capitulate. It was unpleasant to contemplate that principles could be compromised so easily by persons who stood to lose nothing but an honorary place on a civic commission, while persons whose livelihoods were on the line stood ready to sacrifice everything.

One of the meetings we were called to attend was in

the library auditorium. It was rowdy. Our fears that the commission was ready to break were confirmed. There was to be another meeting in the city council chambers following the library meeting. None of us looked forward to it. Feelings were running high, and the censorship people were especially vocal.

The yelling at the meetings we had held for our own people seemed like child's play now. Our group was coldly indignant when faced with the rudeness which characterized the remarks made by the censorship people. A potential for violence was evident in the crowd that night. There was one commission member, however, who reassured us during the library meeting, and who did much to promote the cause at the crucial council meeting. She faced the hostile audience unflinchingly.

Mrs. Marion Elizabeth Gath, Chairperson of the Richmond Public Library Commission, introduced her plea to the city council with a comment on the real issues in the controversy. She felt that the competence of those who had the responsibility for book selection — the library commission, and through them, the librarian — was at issue. And she felt the survival of intellectual freedom in Richmond was being challenged.

She went on to make a personal testimony:

I am the mother of a seventeen-year-old girl, high school graduate, and I don't think there's any finer child in the whole United States — or the world. The reading has never been censored in our home. My daughter has read a copy of the *Barb*, and we discuss these — quote — lewd, indecent publications — whatever you feel they are or the public feels they are. She is allowed to read what she wants to read. I read it. We discuss the moral values in the publications.

We can not protect our children from everything. We

work. They go to school. They meet all types of people. And I think it's time that parents stop putting the onus of rearing their children on the library, on the school and on the church, and that we take into our own hands our duty and rear our own children.

Everyone must do his own thing. I am a Christian. I rear my child in a Christian manner and read the bible with her — and discuss it with her and instil in her the principles of Christianity. And I am not afraid to let her go anywhere, talk to anyone, or read anything!

Mrs. Gath sat down to the polite applause of the anti-censorship people, who have frequently been thought of as disruptive and irresponsible in their behavior at meetings. The lesson in irresponsible and disruptive behavior was being led by the censors this night. They heckled, booed, hissed and yelled insults whenever something was said which displeased them. Our applause seemed quite inadequate to compensate for the abuse our speakers had to tolerate.

The next speaker, Mrs. Royce Klock, was a pro-censorship organizer. She shocked the meeting by declaring that when she had talked to the librarian, John Forsman, he had sworn at her. In view of the verbal excesses which we were witnessing at the meeting the charge sounded quite serious. Then it was brought out that Mr. Forsman had said the word "Goddamn" during his conversation with her. Our group enjoyed a snicker. Mrs. Klock's speech was hardly a memorable one, except for one catchy phrase she used at the end. "When I see dirt I clean it up!" she said. One could not help wondering if she never felt overwhelmed — she obviously had a talent for seeing dirt where no one else could.

The next speaker was an Episcopal Priest. His name was Lester Kinsalving, a member of the Commission on Legislation and Public Morals of the Northern California Council of Churches. In his introduction he epitomized the

Berkeley Barb as "an enormously colorful, often tasteless, journalistic joke," but he tempered his criticism by stating his opinion that it was necessary to show materials caused direct hurt to people before declaring them obscene. He expressed his concern about the increase in the depictions of violence which were being tolerated while censorship of sexual materials increased.

He went on:

— If you can ban the *Berkeley Barb,* think of what else this group will want to ban!

I can think of one volume right off the bat which has a four-letter word denoting urine, and it appears seventeen times in that one bound volume. There are four passages in this one volume that mention the consumption of human excrement!

There's another passage . . . which is one of the most erotic descriptions you've ever read of the beauties of the naked female breast. And there's another passage which goes into the description of comparing the male sexual organ to that of an animal!

Now this book is being distributed in motel rooms and hotel rooms all over the state by a group called the Gideons.

And if you think this is in any way an exaggeration, a colleague of mine named Arthur Hoppe has written on this and has gotten protests of *The Holy Bible* — because this is all of course in *The Holy Bible.*

During the priest's speech the interruptions from the audience grew in volume, and at one point the gavel had to be used — the speaker had to appeal to the audience to allow him to continue. The laughter which he provoked by some of the comments above — and other humorous anecdotes which we have no room for here — took away some of the seriousness which was beginning to be evident in the calls from the offended censors. The next speaker, who introduced an intellectual-freedom domino theory into the discussion — saying "What will they next elect to bring into the library?" — helped quiet the censors.

But the address of Mr. Henry Ramsey, Jr., Chairman of the Committee on Censorship of the Richmond Friends of the Library was not designed to keep either side quiet. He said:

> We speak in support of the present position of the librarian . . . with regard to the retention of certain publications which have come under criticism.
>
> I think that one can reasonably say that people who find sexual intercourse dirty are sick [laughter from audience] — they're really sick — because it is an enjoyable and pleasurable experience and further it is the principal means which has been provided — as a matter of fact, to date, the only means [laughter] whereby we may reproduce ourselves. That's point one.
>
> Point two [disturbance by Mrs. Strindberg and others, brought to order by the chair] — the human body is not an indecent or filthy thing. It is what we have, and the body that we must use and function with. And I certainly do not feel that there's anything indecent or ugly about it, and people who do — I think that they're sick.
>
> Finally, there's certain normal, natural functions that we perform such as the elimination of human waste — both liquid and solid [laughter] — and in that sense there is nothing filthy or dirty about that.
>
> Those persons that say that God created us — He created us within that manner of eliminating our functions [sic] and I feel that people who find that that's dirty or filthy are sick people. Now I'm not so much concerned about those people that find sex, the human body and the elimination of certain waste materials dirty as I am . . . about other people — in that I do not think that it

is proper for this city to attempt to establish rules that
will contribute to the development of feelings of guilt
within people about what are natural functions: such as
simply existing and *being* with regard to your body; such
as deriving pleasure and perpetuating the race with regard
to sex; and finally with regard to eliminating the natural
bodily functions.

I would say in conclusion that the mere fact that
you have a substantial number of people on both issues
of this question should illustrate to you that this is a
document, publications [sic] and a policy that should
be left alone because we should not have a tyranny of
the majority that should dictate to a minority whether
they are adult or child . . . .

Mr. Ramsey's time was up and he was being shouted
down during the last moments — perhaps the censors were
offended to find that they did not have a monopoly on expressions of homespun genius. The gathering took a little
time to calm down before the next speaker, Mrs. Edith
Paulini, was able to speak.

Mrs. Paulini's introduction was ironical in view of the
previous speaker's comments on the tyranny of the majority.
She said "What do they mean by intellectual freedom? . . .
if we are still democracy, I believe, still means that majority
rules. And if the majority of us feel that this is not good for
children of this age group, then I believe — and I don't feel
it is being a censorship — that it should be barred from the
library."

Mrs. Paulini's lack of awareness of the need for minority
rights in a democracy was equaled only by her insensitivity to
the feelings of persons belonging to minority groups, for she
went on to say:

. . . I have five children . . . I don't think we're
trying to have a contest of who has the most children

. . . but don't you see that *our* home lives are different from the home lives that most of the children that go to the library are exposed to?

We're not fighting for our children! My children's not going to read that trash, and if they do I wouldn't be afraid if they did . . . . But I am afraid for children that come from perhaps illegitimate homes ("ohs" and laughter from parts of the audience), from homes where parents don't care. Yes, laugh! That's the trouble with you, you think everything like this is a big joke!

But here again — getting back to a more serious vein — perhaps children that are not exposed to the decent part of life, that is, only exposed to the seamy side of life, I mean — what are they going to do with this type of education?

It was unfortunate that the speaker was unable to tell the difference between light-hearted laughter and the laughter which is provoked by incredulity. The population of Richmond was at that time approximately 30 percent black, and there was a sizeable slum area made up of people of various minorities and poor white people. Many of these persons had representation in the audience — in fact, two of the speakers who had supported the library up to this point in the meeting had been respected leaders in the black community. Mrs. Paulini's plea to allow her white middle-class values to dictate what reading materials would be available to the rest of the population must have appeared grotesque to everyone except perhaps the members of the censorship group.

Another speaker for the censors was to give us another view of the consciousness of a member of the black community, however:

My name is Olivera Luckett . . . I'm a community worker at the South Side Center. I also supervise fifty-two youths. I did not come here tonight to make a speech, but after being a youth supervisor I feel like that I should say something because I work with youth every day, and I'm sure some of the youth I work with are here tonight. And I will be frank with me! [sic] I don't think that this issue's really all in trying to protect our children, but mostly in keeping the *Bar* [sic] in the library.

And I think we're here considering our youth, and not about keeping the *Bar* — you know they're more worried about that than about what's going on at the library. I'm gonna tell you what I think about it! I think as a mother of four children and a grandmother, I think — and I'm very proud, I think I'm a young grandmother, which I'm very proud of — a four-week-old grandson, I think I'm real proud of that! And I have children from nine to twenty-five years old. And I'll be frank — from twenty-three to twenty-five I had a very good time raising them. But these last three I cannot speak of that because so many things have gone on since I've been raising (them) — they question me about things they should not question me because — do you know where they get it at? They get it at the library and at different other places.

. . . It might be funny, Mr. Bates [refering to a man laughing in the audience], but you as a . . . probation officer — I don't feel like you should be in favor of such filth that go on! Maybe you call me an old-timer, but I can tell you one thing, I would rather be old-timer than to put out the junk that I see that's on this paper here. And I would not call it no moral because that is nothing to show any young people.

Now, first of all, everybody know sex is beautiful — all of us know, because that's what we came here by — so that's nothing to talk about. But what I'm speaking of — to put it out here — why don't you bring it to the city council and put it out . . . here? That's what you all say we should do. There's nothing wrong with it. So just bring it up here to the girls and boys here!

Tell them it's all right for them to have sex right up

here! That's what I think we should do because of the way you all feel — and the people sitting here laughing: "I've brought my girls — I'll let them do this!"

Well I'll tell you about *me*. If I ever catch one of *mine* reading such filth [laughter and yells of encouragement from the audience] I'd beat 'em to death, almost . . . [the reaction of the audience forces a pause]. Because I think it is filth . . . and I think that for a librarian to get up and speak on such a thing and people set up and laugh about it — . No, they don't like what I'm saying because, *yes*, I'm ole-time because I was raised a moral way and I feel if everyone else was raised a moral way they wouldn't speak this kinda thing. No, I was raised in a Christian home, and my mother didn't know — they didn't talk this thing — maybe they shoulda told me more about it! But I tell you one thing, I'm glad today that they didn't because I can raise and teach my kids right from wrong . . . .

What would a nine- or ten-year-old child know about that book that's placed in the library? They don't know any more about that than they'll go back on the streets and tell what they've bought . . . .

I'm just up here to speak on something that I think is right, because I work with youth every day and I'm not down there teaching those youth that it is all right for them to do anything they want to do, because it is not all right. And I don't feel that a mother should teach that. And I'm not just speaking for one mother, I'm speaking for all the mothers . . . in Richmond, because I feel like they appreciate me telling their children right from wrong.

But I'll tell you they're teaching them so much now even I disagree even in the schools the things that they are teaching to them, because they come home and tell you about birth control and all this kinda junk [yells of encouragement from audience], and that's why so much is going on now, the kids know so much. Seven and eight years old, they can tell you anything! I tell you all you need to do is ask them a question and I'll tell you they can answer it for you . . . .

Richmond wouldn't be all tore up like it is if you all had the ole-time raising — wouldn't have all this dope and stuff in Richmond, I tell you for sure. [Applause]

We got some of everything in Richmond. We have dope addicts, we have all kinds of drunks and stuff on the streets with our twelve- and thirteen-year-old kids. You all know this — no use you all trying to lie and say you don't know it — you all know about this dope in Richmond!

Mrs. Luckett had been a very fast speaker — witness the amount of information she managed to pack into her time. The timekeeper had allowed her a minute and a half beyond the agreed-upon three minutes. The rapidity of her delivery and the unfamiliar syntax she used made me think I should add myself to the list of dopes in Richmond! Mrs. Luckett had given us a lot to think about.

The calm, measured tones of the assistant staff counsel of the American Civil Liberties Union of Northern California was now heard — but the audience had been aroused by the previous speaker and there was little chance that the censors would allow an opposing voice to be heard. The gavel had to be used repeatedly to allow the speaker to be heard. A man identified with the John Birch Society continued to call "Throw him out!" during the period the ACLU representative was able to speak.

I come to speak in favor of the first amendment to the United States Consitution   [boos], which provides that Congress shall make no law abridging freedom of speech [noisy disturbances throughout the hall], and through the fourteenth provides that no state or local government shall abridge freedom of speech.

And what we are talking about is freedom of speech — the content of particular periodicals. Now — the most offensive form of censorship is prior censorship, that is, censorship by which you determine before literature is exposed whether you like it or don't . . . and then don't permit it to be circulated. That's especially true when you decide that a periodical *in perpetuum* must be banned because it at one time expressed views you don't like.

Now there's been a lot of talk about the *Berkeley Barb* and other magazines as if they were obscene. If they were in fact obscene — or if they are in fact obscene in any issue — they can be prosecuted — anybody who exhibits them — under [Section] 311 of the penal code. That's how we punish the purveying of obscene matter in California, after it's distributed.

The exhibitor may be prosecuted, or the person who is selling it may be prosecuted. And if the *Barb* is really obscene I assume it would have been prosecuted in Richmond and that your district attorney and police force have not been remiss in their duties . . . .

I don't think respect for law and order is going to be engendered by running rough shod over the Constitution of the United States. If we don't have respect [loud disturbances are being made in the audience] for our basic laws we're not gonna have respect for any laws. And that basic law says this: that we don't have a paternalistic country, and we especially don't have it in the form of a government [yelling from audience and repeated calling for order and gaveling by chair] — that decides what's good for people to read or decides that the only literature available ought only be that suitable for children . . . .

With that the disturbances became so severe it was evident the meeting could not continue. The council held a hurried consultation and decided to meet with the library commission and the librarian to decide the issue.

During the meeting council member G. Vargas had made it evident that he was in sympathy with the censors, saying "Don't anybody get the idea that this council can't do anything, because we have the final determination what should be purchased — and we have the determination to fire the commission — and we have the right, if there's anything wrong!" He had been responsible, a number of times during the meeting, for bringing the discussion away from the principles involved in order to make remarks which reflected on individuals, especially the librarian.

He drew attention to the fact that one woman had complained about swearing and said, "If our librarian or any one on the commission is talking to any one of our people in the city the way these people have been telling me, then I'm for firing the whole bunch!" His statement was followed by enthusiastic "yeh"s and applause from the censorship group in the audience.

It was little wonder that the people who had stood against the censors felt gloomy about the outcome — their advocates had been silenced, and the issue was out of their hands.

The meeting had been recorded for radio broadcast by the Pacifica radio station KPFA (and the recording was subsequently issued by Pacifica Archive Records under the title *What Shall They Read?*). The radio reporter interviewed a number of people at the close of the meeting, including librarian John Forsman. John was understandably down at the mouth:

> It has been a great loss for librarianship so far. I thought the city council would stand on the right of professional librarianship and on the rights for the freedom of choice. But instead they bowed to public pressure as they often do — which is what always happens when you bring book selection into a public arena . . . . They should have learned their lesson that they are going to have this happen to them every time, over and over and over again, until they take all book selection out of the political arena.

As there is an election going on shortly, after the election — I think — it will calm down. That's my hope anyway.

Reporter: You do feel that the *Avant Garde, Berkeley Barb* and the *Los Angeles Free Press* are of value in the Richmond Public Library?

They certainly are, or I wouldn't have put them there in the first place — and I'll stand behind it all the way!

The next person to be interviewed was Mrs. Dorothy Strindberg, one of the women who had brought the matter before the council:

My opinion of what has happened tonight is, *HALLELUJAH, Bless the Lord* for giving me the guidance to come up and *fight* for the youth of my community and decency and righteousness! That is what I said tonight.

Reporter: But there's been no final decision —

Mrs. S.: The final decision was made when I seen the people come here tonight to support me.

Reporter: In the end do you think —

Mrs. S.: I am not overconfident! I feel that it may take a little while to gain the point, but we did gain the interest, and that's what counts!

I was the final person to be interviewed. If I had known that my voice would be used to sum up the matter in a recording which would have nationwide distribution, I might have used better grammar!:

I am . . . former city librarian of Roswell, New Mexico, where we had a censorship issue very similar last fall . . . . We had the same stereotyped speeches by the same kind of people, and it took the same pattern of becoming personal against the librarian and his family — and against the board. And we eventually won — we thought — the board supported us, all of the professional organizations supported us. But the viciousness from that small minority in the community was so bad that eventually my wife and I left. They have as yet no librarian . . . I don't think they will find one in a long time . . . .

This tears down a community. After all, the librarian is not out corrupting children on the streets and has no intention of doing so. And when these groups get after a person who is an educated person and who has good intentions towards the community, when they run him out of town other people start running out of town. Good people don't come back into town and it is a loss for the whole community.

Not long after that meeting was held we heard that the Richmond Library Commission had reversed itself and capitulated to the censors. We had left the northern California area by this time, as I had business in Los Angeles, but we kept in touch. We understood that John Forsman was placed in a difficult position by the commission's decision, since he was bound to obey them in policy matters and bound to support intellectual freedom by his professional principles. His health had started to suffer, and he had justifiably developed a cynicism about the value of the sacrifices he had made for an ungrateful community. He resigned, and the Richmond Library — labeled as a censorious institution within the library profession — spent a lengthy time without the services of a head librarian.

John joined the ranks of the happy-go-lucky "dissident spokesmen" of the profession, and was fortunate to find good positions in subsequent years, eventually teaching library science to new library recruits. Unfortunately his students were likely to face the jobhunting nightmare that had first made itself evident to the librarians who had been victims of censorship. We were discovering that there were more librarians than there were jobs. The future was looking more uncertain for many people — John had been lucky.

23

Dirty Old Man

June and I — and our dog Shandy — got by okay.

I finally succeeded in finding a library job. I became head librarian of a "township," a political subdivision smaller than a county. It included four communities and a small rural area with a population of approximately thirty thousand. It was in Illinois, about an hour's drive from Chicago.

It was a smaller responsibility than Roswell had been, in a smaller, more decrepit library building. My office this time was behind the boiler in the basement. The Scottish motif was here again (although Carnegie had not been given an opportunity to visit his largesse upon these communities): the township was called Dundee, after the industrial city in eastern Scotland.

But the heritage of the citizens of Dundee was just as diverse as many another American community — at least in terms of mixed European ancestry. They had an historical awareness of their own origins, but their proximity to Chicago had kept this from developing into narrow conservatism. The one thing their forefathers had not handed down to them was a good library. There were people who wanted one, however.

The library building was a mediocre, picturesque, ancient structure with hardly a claim to historical importance or architectural significance, but because it stood high on a hillside it seemed impressive. Before the library had been located there it had been someone's home for over eighty years! Members of the community were very fond of citing our beautiful, "historic" building as an excuse for our lack of a proper library facility. It did not matter that the space was inadequate, the stairs dangerous and the eaves crumbling.

The job was one of those where you say you were motivated to take it "because of the challenge" rather than admit "there are overwhelming problems but I can't find anything better."

There were certain positive things that could be said about the job. The board of trustees was well motivated. They had no prejudiced view of my past (it was necessary to acquaint them with the Roswell affair to protect my own future as well as their interests). I did not go around expecting to be confronted with a censorship issue.

The staff was a congenial group of non-professional women who had learned their library skills the hard way through the tutelage of a tartar (the previous librarian) who had monitored their every move. I therefore had the benefit of an appreciative, disciplined staff prepared to love me for allowing them to do their jobs independently.

There was one other good thing about taking the job at Dundee: it allowed me to enjoy living in one of the prettiest areas of the Midwest. It was located in the heart of rolling, green, partly wooded countryside, and it had the benefits of closeness to the city with the relaxed feeling of country living. It would have been an excellent place for outdoor living if the extremes of Midwestern weather hadn't constantly interfered. The threat of tornadoes was bad enough, but I learned especially to hate the cold in winter.

In the library I tried to face the challenge of making the existing structure useful while agitating for a new building. It soon became obvious there would be no new building unless we overcame the hostile competitiveness between the various communities. It is a strange-but-true story that there had once been an attempt to resolve intercommunity rivalry by placing a new library between them on a bridge in the middle of the river which separated them. There were numerous reasons why the attempt failed, but one of the factors involved, reportedly, was an opinion held by some that the bridge would simply offer more opportunities for members of the other communities to confront one another!

There was little else to do to improve things after I had rearranged the interior, improved staff work schedules, started a program of purchasing materials to make the collection interesting, and struggled to gain sympathy for improved staff salaries and more professional help.

And so I found that I had time to take on other challenges, for although the library sometimes took sixty hours of my time a week, it certainly wasn't as demanding as Roswell had been. My first project outside the library was to attempt to establish a group of community-conscious, people-oriented, censorship-hating library workers who would take on the Chicago area and possibly the whole state, to raise library consciousness. Others felt the need too. I became coordinator of a group which called itself the Illinois Social Responsibilities Round Table (ISRRT!). We were an affiliate of the American Library Association.

This proved to be fun. The radical consciousness hadn't quite filtered to the general population in the Midwest yet — at least in terms of style — and our group could talk of radical social change without the bitterness and personality clashes of groups elsewhere. We didn't care that we were sometimes called the *"bourgeois"* by members of the so-called New York-Philadelphia Axis of library militants. We could evaluate our own motives and allegiances. The group was a good influence on me.

We were doing as much or more than some of the self-professed militant groups. We tried to change people's attitudes towards library service. We had task forces to collect books for a library for American Indian children, to investigate censorship, to modify library education, and to look into the library services offered prisoners in the jails. We had provocative programs each month, and librarians from the entire Chicago area (and anyone else, for that matter) were invited to attend.

We had some crazy programs, such as the time we invited the editors of the two major underground newspapers in the city, the *Chicago Seed* and the *Second City* to talk to us. We had only been vaguely aware that there was considerable enmity between the two. Their differences stemmed from an ideological base, one being anarchist, the other socialist.

When the evening of the meeting arrived, June and I had to drive into the city to pick up the editor of the *Seed*. He was bleary-eyed from having stayed up all of the previous night to cover the Black Panther police raid. He was very bitter about the actions of the Hanrahan-led police. He told us of the evidence he had seen which indicated the shootings had been murder by the law officers.

The editors were soon busy giving our audience a review of the purposes of their presses. Each was interested in his own programs and wanted to promote his own political viewpoint, it was soon evident. They had little awareness that the librarians they were addressing had an interest of their own in social change. What started out as banter between the two soon descended to namecalling. The audience learned little about how the newspapers could help their public, but they received an education in ideology. I'm sure a number had been unaware — until then — that anarchy and socialism are irreconcilably opposed. It gave a number of "liberals" cause to question their own acceptance of some of the bases of their own beliefs. "It was a helluva show!" one of them said to me afterwards, and I took it as a compliment. It was too bad the entertainment had been at the expense of one dedicated idealist who was near the point of exhaustion.

Our meetings soon became routine. Union organizers, sex education promoters and censorship victims all spoke to us. We were soon being asked by the national Social Responsibilities Round Table to provide programs for visiting groups of librarians. One of our first efforts in this direction involved an attempt to find alternative lodgings for conventioneers at the American Library Association's midwinter meeting. Many delegates were believed to object to the use of hotels which were controlled by monopolist white interests.

I became the coordinator of the "Roberts Motel Project," (named for the black-owned motel which we planned to use to house our people). We spent many hours working on that, making sure that the facilities were adequate, arranging for transportation between the location and the conference hotels, coordinating the registration process and arranging financial matters. But the project suffered from our usual failing, being long on ambition, ideals and rhetoric and short on action. Few delegates to the convention really wanted to stay in a black-owned motel some distance from the conference.

The project failed, and after the disappointment it was good to get back to the library and get busy with routines. There was plenty of work to be done. We had an appreciative staff and a growing number of adherents in the community. This retreat — the Dundee community — was a nice, middle-class, white surburban area. Principles be damned — sometimes we need a place where our presence won't be questioned.

I liked getting back to the decrepit old building and cheerful staff. I wrote letters to the disappointed conference delegates who had signed up for the project and then settled back into the library routines.

We had new services at the library. We obtained magazines on microfilm to conserve storage space. We purchased a sound movie projector to loan to people to show the films they were able to reserve through us. We got special reading lamps with magnifier lenses attached for those who had difficulty reading. We bought large print books, rented a second copying machine for public use, and even installed a better sidewalk outside the building. We bought paperbacks to appeal to everyone.

For the young people we bought recordings, put up special displays, hung posters on the walls, and even acquired a special collection of bound comic books.

The comics were one of the most popular collections ever. Even after we owned nearly eight hundred volumes of the comics it was difficult to find more than a couple of dozen in the library at any one time. They ranged from *Beetle Bailey, Superman* and *Donald Duck* to the literary classics. Today's parents were brought up on such things, and they don't seem to have inherited the fear that such materials can damage the mind — many were happy just to see their kids becoming more enthusiastic about visiting the library. The kids usually took some ordinary books — and records — with them, too.

It was the young people who made the Dundee experience most worthwhile. Some children got in the habit of asking for me and trooping down to my office. One little girl used to come in and — after a suitable exchange of pleasantries and some summary information about what she was doing at school — would ask if she could please rummage through my waste basket. She loved the old commercial book catalogs, discarded posters and the like.

"How come you are throwing away such *good* junk?" she would ask. The staff got in the habit of announcing her by saying "Here comes someone looking for good junk. Got any today?"

The young people who made the greatest impression

were those hired from the high schools as library pages. We usually had about ten of them, and most of them were girls (boys still don't apply for library positions very often, unfortunately). The bookish, studious-looking schoolgirl was hardly evident (at least as far as appearance went). Although we had many intelligent, well educated young people working for us, they all had a spark of fun in them, a spontaneity.

The pages assisted in the selection of popular recordings, for instance, as well as doing the routine library chores. At one time we even had some pages and their friends involved enough in what we were trying to accomplish in the library that they wanted to sponsor a rock concert to begin a building fund for the library. Needless to say, the adults who maintained the tea-party image of library support, who helped guide the library's policies — and upheld community antagonisms — soon quashed that.

The kids were inclined to be irresponsible about their work schedules on occasion. But youthful enthusiasms do dictate headstrong actions which may jeopardize the routine activities of one's life — I can still testify to such urges myself. I had to clamp down sometimes in order to keep the plant going. Even the lack of one semi-skilled library page can disrupt library operations to a serious extent. The library staff still thought I was soft on the youngsters, and it may have been true.

I guess I didn't help matters when it was brought to my attention that some of the girls were wearing extremely abbreviated hot pants to work. I said that since we were technically not supposed to be using our young ladies for clerical tasks (although we were doing so), we could hardly insist that they dress for a clerical position — especially since we paid them so little. They often had to climb small ladders or bend to the lower bookshelves. They carried many heavy bundles of books each work day. It got quite hot in the library during the summer. They should be permitted to dress comfortably and informally, I thought.

I announced that I had no particular prejudice about the clothes worn by my employees — as long as they were serviceable, reasonably neat, and not likely to cause a disruption because of patron response to excessive nudity. "In case of a report of excessive nudity," I said, chuckling, "the girls should be sent immediately to me in my office behind the boiler in the basement. There I can examine the evidence in private and discuss her problems intimately."

No complaints about the girls' dress were received after that, although the threat didn't appear to have inhibited any of the young set in their choice of clothing. Perhaps the staff had some fear that I might be serious about that intimate conference. I was delighted when the pages got together some time later and bought me a T-shirt which had written on it in bold letters "DIRTY OLE MAN!"

24

Chicago

The meetings of our group and its task forces continued. I was attending two or three meetings of the group a month, in addition to all of the library-related meetings I had to attend. It was very demanding, but I felt it was worth it.

The group received a request from "national" to provide an alternative program during the association's conference in Chicago. We met together to discuss the possibility of adding something significant to the usually dull programs. People would be coming from all over the nation. People with that much dedication deserved to go home with more to remember than discussions of cataloging and votes on the use of association funds.

It took us a lengthy meeting time to come up with an acceptable subject for a program — and then it happened in a negative way.

"They shouldn't be having conventions in Chicago," somebody said.

"Why — because of the weather?"

"No. Because of what happened in Chicago at the Democratic Convention in 1968."

The incident referred to had occurred before my arrival

185

in the Chicago area. Many people had gathered to protest
the American involvement in the Vietnam war, and during
the demonstration many — including innocent bystanders
— had been injured in what an official investigation later
called a "police riot." Following the confrontation between
the demonstrators and police the authorities had compounded
the offense by initiating police raids on the hotel rooms of
youthful convention delegates — the surprised young people
were severly roughed up by vengeful officers, although many
of them had had nothing to do with the previous event.

"They don't call this town Pig City for nothing," a prim
looking middle aged lady said, surprising us. "My son was
on the way home from the YMCA that night and was clubbed
by policemen who were looking for just any young people to
beat up!"

I wondered if there might be something in the conversation which would help us find a proper subject for our
"significant" meeting. "There have been a couple of attempts
to get the association to vote to stop holding meetings in
Chicago," I said, "but the membership turned the idea
down."

"They figure nobody's going to beat up on little old
librarians anyway."

The comment jogged my memory, for I remembered a
documentary film I had seen which had shown the police
roughing up a nice old lady who might have been anybody's
idea of a librarian (she happened to have been Anne Kerr,
a visiting British member of parliament who managed to get
in the way of the police). The film had shown much of the
brutality and the excesses which had occurred at the Democratic convention. I mentioned it to the group. "If I could
get hold of that film and show it — would that make a
suitable program?" I asked.

"You're damn right it would!" an overenthusiastic

librarian yelled (I wondered momentarily about the sound level in his public library). Moments later I had been assigned the task of finding the film. Someone else had been assigned the task of locating a hall where the film could be shown. Another person had been "volunteered" to handle the publicity after we had confirmed the details.

I reflected that we could be quite efficient — between bouts of rhetoric — when we had a specific task to address ourselves to. All we had to do was find the people who were already too busy and assign the tasks to them. Unfortunately, I fitted the description of a person who was already too busy — and there was the additional complication of the many miles I had to drive each time I visited the city.

"Will you introduce the film and chair the discussion afterwards?" somebody asked me as an afterthought. My mouth fell open and I started looking around the room, my finger half extended, searching for someone else to take this added burden. I could see heads hurriedly turning away. "Good! I knew we could rely on our good old, hard working coordinator!" the same voice said.

"Sucker!" I said to myself under my breath.

When the week of the conference came I had a miserable dose of 'flu. We had received an unofficial "friendly" warning from a librarian who had contacts with the Chicago police that they were aware of our proposed meeting and that we'd best behave ourselves. If there were any demonstrations or the like we should beware of provocateurs from the police department. We'd also had some difficulty with the people in charge of the auditorium we were going to use (it was in the main building of the Chicago Public Library) who were very insistent that we pre-screen the film "to see that it runs o.k. and doesn't have any tears." I decided to ignore the message which purported to come from the police, and to refuse to pre-screen the film on principle, since I had a concern that the library might try to censor it. I was not easy in my mind.

It seemed that half the people in the Midwest had the 'flu. My library had been operating under a severe strain because of the number of workers who were ill. The only thing that saved us was the number of library patrons who were also confined to bed.

The conference had been going for a couple of days when I finally felt well enough to travel into Chicago and take a hotel room there (I was not yet fit enough to face commuting back and forward). The film showing was scheduled for the next day.

I had hardly been at the conference hotel an hour when I was handed a strange pamphlet which purported to publicize our program. Our own publicity had already been distributed. It had been a straightforward announcement of time, place, sponsoring agency and program. This new pamphlet had been picked up by one of our people from a bundle left in the hotel lobby. It was graphically arresting, and started by inviting people to join a march for peace which would end at the library auditorium at the time we had arranged. It then went on to describe the program at the auditorium as a "SPIRO AGNEW MEMORIAL CENSORSHIP PARTY . . . IN GOOD OLD PIG CITY," and it ended with the words "*sponsored by yippie!*"

My knees felt a little more weak after I had read it. It wasn't quite the accepted style of publicity used to inform librarians of a serious program on the subject of social responsibility and community awareness. None of our people knew of the pamphlet's origins — but they did know it had already received wide distribution. I imagined that some of the more radical group members from the East Coast had grown dissatisfied with our staid Midwestern efforts and had decided to liven things up without consulting us. "The New York-Philadelphia Axis strikes again!" I said.

Our group then got into a huddle and decided the measures which would be taken to disclaim responsibility for this unwanted publicity. There was a possibility that otherwise our program would not be allowed to continue at the public library.

When I flopped into the hotel bed that night, besotted by aspirins for my cold and whisky for my head, I reflected that the program would at least gain the attention of busy conference people now. But it kept crossing my mind that the escapade might well have sabotaged our entire effort. There were many less worthwhile meetings being held at the conference — why did our house radicals have to risk the programs which came nearest to accomplishing their own ends?

The next day dawned cold but sunny. My condition had improved somewhat, and I could anticipate facing the crowd at our program without fear of losing my voice. There was still a little annoyance to keep me from taking the success of the program for granted — the persons who regulated the use of the auditorium at the Chicago Public Library had been asking for precise identification of the group which would be presenting the program. I guessed that the strange publicity of the previous day had something to do with the request, so I hastened to assure them of the name of our group and its local membership. And I reasserted that the program was open, free of charge, to all members of the public and the library profession who might be interested (I was under the impression that such gatherings in a public auditorium had to be open to all).

When I got down to the auditorium with the can of film there were a number of people there already, although there were more than thirty minutes to go before the program started. In addition to a few librarians that I could identify, and a few other strangers, there were two library guards and two men in the uniforms of the Chicago Police Department. There were probably plainclothes officers about too, but I was unable to identify any of these among the library patrons, tourists and meeting-goers in the area. I wasn't too reassured, being uncertain of the intentions of the law-and-order people as much as of the radicals. The city officers remained inconspicuous, browsing in the display cases outside the auditorium.

Soon the "march" from the conference arrived with its contingent of library press representatives as well as librarians. They seated themselves quietly. Three young people had come in at about the same time. They were dressed in strange costumes and carried bundles wrapped in brown paper. They stood around the doors of the place, sometimes browsing in the display cases outside when people appeared to be taking notice of them. It seemed odd that the police officers and the youths would consort in such an activity — although it was notable that they chose different cases to gaze into.

The auditorium was a dark, gloomy place with a high ceiling and hard, wooden, straight-backed seats. I gave a brief message of welcome and introduction, then gave the signal to the projectionist to start the film.

The film was a documentary compiled from news film and other sources for the American Civil Liberties Union. Soon we were watching the 1968 disruption, and I could feel myself tense as the familiar scenes unfolded. The audience was similarly gripped.

I could feel the weakness from the influenza combining with the anxiety of the circumstances surrounding the film program, and I knew I should not have come — I could easily have handed over the responsibility to someone else. The sharp, clipped tones of the police officers ordering the crowds to disperse during the demonstration seemed to cut through my entrails.

I consoled myself with the thought that I was probably

the only one who had noticed the Chicago cops in the outer hallways. The library guards, also uniformed, were inside the doors, watching the film. As the mayhem in Grant park was flashed onto the screen I wondered how they felt. I asked myself why I had suddenly begun to feel more threatened by the forces of law and order than by anything else. The screen gave the answer.

The film showed the lady from the British parliament being thrown brutally into the paddywagon. Then — just as we had been ready to conclude that they had done their worst — the camera showed a policeman spraying mace through the door of the vehicle onto the prostrate woman. The producers of the film had included a small interview with the woman, but her recollections of it all seemed anti-climactic, the film had been so graphic. Soon we had passed to other memorable scenes — a girl being dragged along the ground by her hair, a man being kicked by the police while he lay on the ground — it was almost too much to take.

Suddenly my attention was drawn to the back of the room. The young people were moving about, whispering to people in the audience. They had apparently given some of the members of the audience paperback books under some pretense — the books had been in the parcels they carried. Now they seemed to want to discuss the books — and some members of the audience weren't appreciating it. The film droned on, with most of the audience trying to concentrate on the screen. I rather welcomed the opportunity to give my attention elsewhere, although I would have preferred a non-anxiety-producing circumstance.

The film ended and I tried to get people to react to what they had seen or discuss what was important to them. "Let's rap!" I said. I could see the young people still involved in discussion with various members of the audience. The young men were wearing robes, and had some kind of signs around their necks, and the young woman was wearing what has been called "Spanish revolutionary" garb and carrying a toy machine gun. The audience's attention was split between me on the platform and the youths. "We seem to have some picketers," I said, noting that the signs said SECRET SERVICE and SPIRO AGNEW. I wondered at the significance of the signs, but could only conclude that they had some connection with the publicity of the previous day. I assured the audience that the young people were not part of the group which had arranged the program.

Suddenly there was yelling from the back part of the room. "Filth!" "Dirty books!" "What are you librarians doing with obscenity?" "You are all rotten, all of you!" It was the young people prancing up and down the central aisle. Two of them had grabbed paperback books out of the hands of the surprised librarians and were tearing them up, throwing the pages into the air. "How could you read this awful stuff?" one of them yelled, "Do you know what it does to your mind?"

The library guards were advancing on them, but they didn't seem to be aware of it. "Pigs!" One of the young men yelled, but I don't think he was referring to any of the guards or policemen. "There's four letter words here!"

With that the auditorium doors opened and the city police looked in inquiringly. "What's happening?" one of them asked me, since I was at the front of the hall near the door he had entered. I pointed dumbly to the confusion at the other end of the auditorium, and the policemen lost no time in joining the library guards who were herding the young people together. Within seconds the youngsters were handcuffed and being led away.

"Help us, man!" one of them said as they were being shoved out the door. "Don't let the pigs get us!"

There was a stunned silence for a moment. "Does anyone

know what happened?" I asked. A babble of voices broke out. It was some minutes before we were able to piece together the story. The Yippies (for that is what they claimed to be) had let a few people know what they were going to do — but they hadn't felt that it was necessary to inform the organizers of the program. Apparently organizers of any kind were considered to be too authoritarian — their own efforts excepted, of course. They had been putting on a guerilla theatre presentation for us.

Our informant said that the presentation had originally been meant to demonstrate the irrationality of censors. They hadn't realized the thrust of the film's message until it was too late and they were committed to the censorship thing. They had ended up instead reinforcing the message of the film — there wasn't a person in the room who wasn't partially traumatized by the arrests which had happened in front of their eyes seconds after viewing the beatings on the screen. That it was our play-acting "censors" who were arrested was an inconsistency which most of the audience was inclined to overlook.

After the babble of voices had calmed down and the facts of the matter seemed to have become clear there wasn't much more to say. A couple of voices were heard trying to assess blame for what had happened — and I was the butt of their remarks — but the general concern for the welfare of the young people was uppermost in the minds of most people. "What do you think has happened to the kids?" someone asked.

"I wonder if there's anything we can do to help?" I said. "Anybody got any ideas?"

The door swung open and a librarian who had been in the audience earlier walked into the room. "I went down with the police," he said. "They've taken the kids down to the city librarian's office where they are calling for a wagon.

They are to be taken to jail and booked for disturbing the peace."

A number of people turned to me. "You organized this thing," one of them said, "Can't you do something? Can't you have them freed?"

Somebody else said, "They didn't do any damage, and they meant no harm." The audience, which a few moments ago had been scared and confused, was now being drawn together in a bond of sympathy for the youths. But there was one negative note. A friend of mine, a person I had helped on a number of occasions, but who had pretenses of radical social concern which verged on the irrational, jumped forward and pointed a finger at me.

"You are responsible for this!" he said. "You organized this meeting and you didn't leave time in your program for the free expression of revolutionary ideas! You're a goddamn middle-class authoritarian s.o.b. — you better git — "

I didn't hear what else he had to say, as I felt that time was being wasted on his theatricals while the youths might still have some chance of being released. But while I walked down the hallway towards the librarian's office I was burning. I knew the fellow who had made such a show of revolutionary zeal would be acting as if nothing had happened the next time we met in private — he would sue for recognition of our great friendship and apologize profusely if I challenged him. I knew him of old. I reflected that it was his type which precipitated purges in revolutionary movements. I had the uncharitable thought that if I was ever in a revolution with him I would see that he was liquidated before the rest of us suffered. But meantime I would have to watch him when I got back to the auditorium, with or without the young people.

There was a mob of people outside the librarian's office, and I had difficulty approaching the library guard who stood outside the door and kept people from entering. The conversation of the people around was subdued but angry. "Clear the passageway!" the guard kept saying, but no one paid any attention. "Come on now, clear the passageway!" he said again. I recognized some of the people as members of the audience for our program.

I identified myself to the guard, but was at first refused admission. People in the corridor started to murmur about the refusal to allow me to enter. Voices began to be raised. "Let him in!" "He can help them!" "He organized the program — if anyone can talk for them, he can!" The guard began to look uncomfortable, and eventually pushed open the door and consulted with someone inside.

After a few moments he turned to me and nodded, and I was allowed to enter. The scene inside was no more reassuring than that in the lobby. The three culprits were up against the window at the back of the room, still handcuffed, and the two city policemen stood nearby. Office workers sat at the various desks, talking to other employees. All had a uniformly serious look on their faces. They were waiting for the city librarian, someone informed me — he had been called from a meeting in another part of the building, and was expected momentarily. He would decide if charges were to be pressed.

I breathed a little easier when I heard that the decision had not yet been made to press charges. I walked over to the young people and the policemen, hoping to create some kind of communication and open up a way to ease the situation, but before I got there one of the policemen stepped forward and said "Stay back, buddy!"

As I hesitated one of the youths said "We're okay —"

"Shut up!" snapped the policeman.

I stepped back to where I wouldn't present an overt threat to the policeman and waited for the arrival of the city librarian. The people in the room seemed overwhelmed by some mysterious depression as the moments ticked by and the librarian failed to appear at the door.

Then he was there — a little man (I consider myself small at five-foot six, but he was considerably smaller). I had met him before and had been impressed by the mannerisms he apparently used to compensate for his lack of stature. Now they seemed ineffective. The policemen were stealing his thunder by their silent presence. However, after his identity had been made known to the policemen their manner changed to one of deference, and he was back in authority again. Now he used his techniques to the full — he whirled this way and that, asking questions, jabbing a finger, making veiled accusations. Of his assistant: "Do you know who they are — have they been in the library before?" The assistant had no knowledge. He whirled again. "Who brought them in?" The policemen jumped to claim that honor, but that wasn't what he had meant.

He turned to me and snapped, "Are you the one responsible for the program upstairs?" My dumb nodding was exactly the kind of homage he aspired to, and I hated myself for not thinking of a way to be more self-assertive in the face of his aggressive questioning. "Did they have a right to be at your meeting?"

"Yes," I said, "everyone had a right to be there — it was a public meet —"

"That's not what I meant, did you invite them?"

"I invited everybody — "

He was whirling now to question the policemen and staff members, asking questions about damage to property and unnecessary noise in the library.

I managed to gain his attention. "I want to inform you that there's a roomful of irate librarians in that auditorium right now who are very concerned that these young people be released. They want to discuss what has happened. If anyone can tell you what went on, it is them. They want the kids back — "

He was whirling again. He had a brief, whispered conference with his assistant, and they were looking at me and nodding. I half expected to find myself under arrest with the kids, although I couldn't think why. He completed his interrupted whirl and was facing the policemen. "It is okay to let them go," he said.

"No charges?"

"No charges."

The youths were smiling as the policemen unlocked the handcuffs. The officers made no effort to conceal their haste as they left the office. There was a library guard in the room and one outside the door (we could hear the crowd outside the door mumbling as the policemen left), and I guessed they felt a little let down and exposed.

The librarian was speaking to me again. The young people had gathered round me and we must have looked imposing. The victory showed in our faces. "You will go up and explain about the release of these young people," he said. "But I don't want these young people speaking at your meeting. They were not properly invited!"

"But it is a public meeting," I said, "anybody can — " But the librarian had whirled around and was now busily in conversation with someone at the other end of the office.

We trooped out of the office, and there was light applause from the few people there. Most had left when the policemen had gone. I led the crowd back up to the auditorium, where the curious and concerned members of our audience remained. There were statements of congratulations, handshakes, and some "Right on"s. Then we all sat down near the stage to discuss what had happened. There was no question about the right of the young people to speak.

They took advantage of their opportunity, and were soon in a discussion about the effectiveness of the message their play had transmitted. One of our group raised a question about the format of the program we had planned — apparently concerned at the lack of structure in this last part of our event. I reassured the audience that it was entirely proper for the meeting to take whatever turn the audience desired as long as their actions did not oppress others. "Those of you who came simply to see the film may want to stay too — when we set this up we hoped to provoke some reaction in you — it is going even better than we'd planned. It was just unfortunate that the organizers weren't informed so that we could have forestalled a little of the ugliness — "

I had said the evil word, *organizer*. My friend and some others were soon yelling at me for my bourgeois need for control.

I tried to reason them out of their *I'm more radical than thou* syndrome. "How the hell would you have had a meeting at all if we hadn't made the arrangements for the hall — if I hadn't got out of my sickbed to pick up the film — there were letters to write. We had to guarantee the proper use of the hall under our organization's name — "

Somebody in the back of the room yelled "Yippie!" A library guard stuck his head in the door, then quickly withdrew. "Come down off your high horse!" another radical yelled at me. "Let everybody do their thing — you don't have to bore us with your justifications — "

"I'm trying to tell you the meeting is yours — " I said, despairingly. The girl had already started into a discussion of why she had carried a plastic machine gun, and it was obvious that the meeting would break into small discussion groups without help from me. I turned to one of my friends who had helped organize the program and who had been backing me up all during the police episode; she was a friend who knew of my Roswell adventure and my various other circumstances. "Do I have to expect to be threatened by right-wingers and left-wingers *all* my life?" I asked. The question went unanswered. The left-wingers were doing their own thing.

After that there was nothing but confusion in my life for a couple of days. It started when a newspaper reporter identified himself from the audience as I started to leave the hall. I had not been aware that the Chicago press had been present. I answered his questions as well as I could. The next day we were treated to a newspaper article which identified me as a leader of the radical wing of the association which had precipitated the whole untoward circumstance. Calls to the newspaper assured us of an immediate retraction — but meantime I had to worry about the effect of the news upon the people in Dundee. They all took the newspaper. Would I still have a job when I got back? The retraction was never published.

Chaos had been evident in the staid meetings of the association since the Chicago Public Library Yippie incident — or so I heard. I was too sick to attend until it was almost all over. One of our group had been able to address the association and made remarks about witnessing oppression by the Chicago police at the program in the library. The librarian of the Chicago Public Library made a speech asserting that no Chicago policeman had been involved (I learned later that the two we had seen had technically been "off duty"), and that no permission had been given to have "nonmembers" at the meeting. His statement really clouded the issue, and made charges of lying inevitable on both sides. I wished he'd looked at his correspondence or at least listened to me when I had made the statements about our meeting being open to all.

There were then questions about the propriety of our group's use of its identification as an affiliate of the association. It was all terribly petty and tedious. And meantime

I might be out of a job. A number of people were concerned in that regard. When I boarded the bus for Dundee, sick, fearful and disgusted, I carried the promise of letters of support from the president of the association and the past president — if they were needed. They had both looked into the matter and found me blameless. But it was a slight consolation for me — my influenza was back with a vengeance, and the whole world looked gloomy. The only consolation I had was in the knowledge that some of the people who had precipitated the nastier parts of the adventure now suffered from the same virulent flu bug. I managed a throaty chuckle.

25

Routines

Back at the library in Dundee life continued much as usual. "A water pipe burst while you were gone and we had to get it fixed," my assistant said. "And we had to find someone else to shovel snow — our regular boy has dropped out." There was a pile of mail to be attended to. It was good to get back to normal problems.

I was glad to be able to involve myself in such matters as arranging a speech about library affairs for a church group, working with the library budget figures so that we'd have the required report ready for the state library, and investigating the comprehensiveness of the library's insurance.

A little boy fell down the library stairs that week, while I was at lunch. The staff managed to locate me and I had the pleasant task of driving him all around the town to the various places where we might find his mother so that we could be assured that he had proper medical attention. I got indigestion. The kid had been romping around and asking for trouble, but I had to be sympathetic.

When I got back to the library one of the staff members wanted advice on how to proceed with the cataloging of some recordings we had acquired. A salesman had been in my office and had left his card — he would try to catch me later. The diversity of the library administration experience never ceased to amaze me.

There were some minor explanations to be made to key people about what had happened at the conference. Few people had read the article, and fewer had believed it. The retraction did not appear in the newspaper, but it didn't matter. I had worried over nothing.

In the year that followed there were other conferences to attend, new library programs to introduce, personnel crises to overcome — and lots of countryside to explore when there was good weather. I still looked forward to the occasional conference or professional meeting, even though it often meant attending boring meetings from eight A.M. until midnight, required lots of homework, and sometimes could offer a threat to one's professional status, as in the Chicago affair. There was enough change in the attitudes of librarians to hope that our work would accomplish some of the necessary reforms. We wrote and presented resolutions, fought those new measures which we thought were regressive, and generally patted ourselves on the back for our altruism.

The conferences were never boring. At one general meeting of the association I sat near a friend who had recently been fired for questioning the propriety of one church's influence upon the education program in the schools in his community. We had hopes that the association could be induced to assist him in his right to continue to work in his library. He had been acting as a responsible citizen in the matter involving the schools, after all.

Some other matter was being discussed when we were shocked to see two uniformed policemen enter the hall and begin to question him. It soon became obvious that they were concerned with his dress. He was wearing a red, white and blue tie. They wanted to know if it had been manufactured from an American flag (he would have been subject to criminal charges if it had). Fortunately it was a store-bought tie, and a double personal crisis was averted — he was having a hard enough time surviving in the face of the repression he had already experienced. I satisfied my suppressed fury by doing what I would normally consider reprehensible — letting a few "Oink, oink" sounds escape as the policemen left. I had no quarrel with the officers who were required to do their job on receipt of a complaint. My frustration grew out of my knowledge that some librarian had seen fit to make the complaint and bring the officers onto the crowded floor of the conference on an errand which could only be destructive.

But we still had our times for fun. At one non-official gathering (again in an eastern city) we discussed reforms and the possibility of expanding the activities of the *Librarians for Peace* group. Such discussions were guaranteed to produce frustrations which could only be relieved by partying. I achieved notoriety at a subsequent party by retiring under a table which had been draped with a voluminous table cover. There I was able to hold court with a few curious individuals who also did not care about conformity. We enjoyed privacy, a modicum of voyeuristic enjoyment from our unusual angle of observation of the party's goings-on, and a most satisfactory proximity to the refreshments (which were on the table above our heads).

We explored some of the philosophical aspects of professional life in depth and chuckled over the efforts of some of the less adventurous party-goers to assign some Freudian motivation to our "withdrawal." I can recommend the under-the-table gambit to anyone who gets tired of standing around chatting with a cocktail glass in hand.

The party must have been remarkable for its inhibitions-releasing qualities. Another group decided to retire to another room and take their clothes off. Only selected people were informed — the matter was whispered to us on one of our forays from beneath the table.

I had a young lady with me when we heard the news. By that time we had almost decided to leave the party because it was getting late and we had early morning meetings to attend. She had offered me the floor of her place to sleep on. When we discovered that the nude-in was being held in the room where we had left our coats it confirmed our resolve to at least fetch our coats.

When we pushed our way past the stern-faced guardian at the door (saying "We know — we know!" in lieu of a password) — expecting to be greeted by all kinds of frolic and laughter — we were instead greeted by an awful silence and stares. We had to laugh. The naked people were the most uncomfortable, embarrassed looking bunch it was possible to imagine.

They sat in distinct rows, hands conspicuously still, faces with artificial half-smiles which did nothing to hide their discomfort. I looked at them and considered that some had reasonably good-looking physiques. But they obviously hadn't had enough to drink yet — or else their experience had sobered them up very quickly.

"You leaving already?" one of them managed to ask relatively nonchalantly.

"Yeah, man, we got other things to do!" I said, and started to escort my companion to the door.

"Dig it!" the fellow returned, nudging the girl who sat next to him with his elbow and being rewarded by a scowl which intimated that he had taken some kind of physical liberty.

We were laughingly leaving the premises when we were accosted by two serious-looking librarians who inquired about the goings-on in the room we had just left.

"They don't have any clothes on," we said.

" — but there's nothing else going on, unfortunately," I added. "It's a bore."

Our interrogators' faces grew longer and longer. "They are going to discredit us all," one of them said.

"What if it gets into the newspapers?" asked the other.

"Baloney!" I said. "It might do the profession some good — change the image!"

"But do we need it changed that way?"

"What if there's publicity — "

I cut in. "Don't worry about it — my sleeping arrangements tonight would make much better newspaper copy," I said. "Anyway, it isn't going to get out unless you report it."

As we turned to leave I said, "Some day I may write a book about it — people need to know that librarians are humans! *Librarians* need to know that librarians are humans."

Then, as I saw their faces growing longer and longer, I decided to reassure them. "Don't worry — your names won't be mentioned!"

I was going to be sorry to leave for Dundee at the end of that meeting. "Did you notice the bellybuttons?" I asked my companion.

26

Pigs

Life back in Dundee was far from boring either. We had been helping at a newly established free school. The parents had gathered together, purchased a building and recruited teachers with the idea that they might provide their children with an unstructured learning environment (the public schools still equated conformity to the school's dress code with teachability). We had enjoyed working with them — the children were a delight and the parents were an agonized bunch of nervous idealists. They had a reason to be nervous. The powers-that-be were attempting to close the school down, citing everything from delinquency to violation of fire codes.

Then there were our efforts to support the peace cause to keep us from betting bored. My wife and I had attended church-sponsored demonstrations which had received the attention of some state police plainclothesmen with cameras. They had photographed everyone who participated, and for good measure had photographed the license plates of our cars. Later, when the room we used for our peace meetings was bombed (it was in the basement of a church) the minister assured me that the investigators who were sent to the church were the same men who had done the photography. Needless to say, no clues were ever found.

I later had to face questions from my library board about whether it was appropriate for me to be seen at demonstrations. Although I was putting in many more hours at the library than they had a proper right to demand, a couple of board members saw fit to question that I might be using library time to further the cause of peace (although they did not put it in such words!).

I was bourgeois enough to want to believe in the good intentions of most "establishment" people (or so some of my radical friends would be likely to have charged) — after all, I represented the establishment myself. Who levied the overdue fines on the free-school children who brought their books back typically late? Me. It didn't matter that I had agitated for an end to fines. I had to implement existing policy. I was the policeman.

I found myself facing some policemen subsequently at a library conference. In Illinois we had heard that the police were making a drive to have a book removed from all the libraries of the state — the Illinois Police Association had circulated a letter to that effect. Attending the American Library Association conference in Los Angeles I found that the police effort was nationwide. Two officers of the International Conference of Police Associations had requested time to discuss the matter with librarians and the Intellectual Freedom Committee had offered them the opportunity.

The book they wanted to ban was *Sylvester and the Magic Pebble*, a profusely illustrated children's book by William Steig. There was hardly a less likely candidate for censorship. All of the characters in the book were depicted as animals of some sort. There was some social message in the actions of the characters, but it could hardly be called revolutionary or controversial. It was just a nice kid's book. But one illustration showed policemen — as nice, friendly pigs.

I had mixed emotions as I heard the policemen speak

— I wanted to reject what they said utterly. The prior publicity, and the letter from the police association, had all shown the police to be depicting the book as an example of the international communist conspiracy at work — or at least as Yippie propaganda. But as I listened to the representatives from the police associations I heard a different story. Maybe they had found out that librarians wouldn't accept simplistic theories of conspiracy and were likely to resist any effort to remove *any* book from their libraries. These policemen were conciliatory. I wanted to hate them anyway.

For what they said was that the police had now grown accustomed to the "pig" epithet, and instead of resenting it and resisting it they were going to adopt the identification cheerfully. "After all," one of them said, "the pig is basically a clean, loyal animal — one of the most intelligent of farm animals — and it serves man diligently." I wanted to yell out "Yes, but it isn't kosher!"

As they talked I could imagine them at some demonstration bashing heads with a grin on their faces as they chanted, "I'm a pig! I'm a pig! I'm a pig!" Give a dog a bad name . . . . I needed to blame the Yippies too, I realized. They coined the phrase, reportedly, at that 1968 Democratic convention which had haunted me since.

The librarians at the meeting were visibly relieved that they were not going to be asked to remove the books from library shelves. They wouldn't even have to put up an argument. The officers said that although they could not speak for all the members of their fraternal organization, we could be assured that policemen were aware of society's fears of a police state. We had no need to be concerned that they would insist on controlling the reading materials of the public.

"As a matter of fact — " one of the officers said, pulling some little boxes from a coat pocket with a flourish, "I want to demonstrate our good will by making some little awards." He showed us tie clasps, watches, pins and other baubles, all carrying a small depiction of a pig. "This shows how proud we are to be known as pigs. We sell a lot of these to our fellow officers."

He turned to the chairman of our meeting. "And I wonder if you would do us the honor of accepting one of these pins and becoming an honorary pig?"

In a moment the chairman and another association officer had been made the recipients of the pig pins. A confrontation between librarians and police had certainly been avoided, but I had the uncomfortable feeling that a number of principles had been trampled in achieving all of this good will.

I decided to do a little test to see how genuine the goodwill was. I strode over to the platform carrying my own "unity" pin — the clenched fist symbol which depicts the strength of the minorities combined, and which is anathema to those who feel their authority threatened. I could see our association officers start to stiffen as they saw me coming. "I wonder if you would do us the honor of becoming an honorary radical and accepting this pin?" I asked.

I saw the officer's eyes turn steely as he looked from me to the pin and then at the audience. There was a glimmer of a smile on his lips as he said "I'll wear it to my very next demonstration." I pinned it on his lapel.

The meeting broke up, and I had the mild satisfaction of knowing that I had brushed some of the sugar coating off the meeting. The officer's reaction had been inconclusive. I wouldn't want to have to test him at the next head-bashing. Our own librarian-honorary-pigs were looking at me in a perplexed manner. I had another meeting to go to — and then that long road back to Illinois. Politics were such a bore!

"There's a party in suite number 346 — " somebody said.

"Race you there!" I said. Then, "Strange — I feel so naked without my pin!"

"What's the matter, afraid your pants will fall down?"

27

Being Subversive

I was in a lawyer's office in Chicago, and a court reporter was tapping away at his machine as I was interrogated. My own lawyers sat nearby to protect my interests — but the lawyer who was "grilling" me for the deposition wasn't letting that hold him back.

The man had been questioning me for some time, and his questions about even such simple things as my past addresses had made my answers seem like admissions of guilt. Now he was ready to get down to the serious stuff. "Have you ever smoked marijuana?" he snapped, staring into my face intently as he spoke.

I was flabbergasted by the question. I was sitting in a hard chair facing a glaring window, and was feeling distinctly uncomfortable. As I hesitated I could see signals from my lawyers. The court reporter paused with his hands poised above the keyboard.

One of my lawyers finally found his voice. "I'd advise my client not to answer that question," he said.

The interrogating lawyer blustered, but he knew the chance to catch me off guard had passed for a time. I was remembering that I had sworn to tell the whole truth — and was suddenly comforted by the realization that I didn't have to answer embarrassing, irrelevant questions.

We were here to discuss what had happened in Roswell during the censorship issue. It had all happened such a long time ago. It was difficult to tell which questions were pertinent. The lawyer had been upset when I had been unable to remember precise dates for things that had happened. His attitude seemed to be that I was deliberately withholding information. I didn't like to think that my honesty was being questioned, and I was beginning to be concerned about the hostility in the question he had just asked about marijuana. The lawyer was still waiting, watching to see if I would take the instructions of my lawyer.

"Will you answer that?" There was a threatening tone in his voice as he spoke.

"I'd like to know what such a question has to do with my administration of a public library?" I said. The court reporter tapped away at his machine.

"I'll ask the questions here!" he snapped back at me. Then he went on to ask me a number of questions about my day-to-day activities. Had I been responsible for the issuance of news releases to the press during my administration? Had I had contacts with various civic groups in the city? The answers to both these questions were "yes." What civic organizations had I belonged to? I answered that I had been a member of Toastmasters International and a Director of the Roswell Community Little Theatre. "No other organizations? What about your memberships now?" I suspected that he was hoping I would admit to being a member of a subversive organization — or at least Gay Liberation or the Organization of Nasty American Nudists. I started to tell him about being the coordinator of the Social Responsibilities Round Table in Illinois, and a member of the Intellectual Freedom Committee of the Illinois Library Association — but he interrupted me.

"Have you ever — " he paused, and his body bent and

tensed like a spring as he turned from the window to face
me. "Have you ever — refused induction into the armed
forces?" he said, spitting out each word forcefully. The
question seemed to be an indictment in itself.

"Don't answer that!" my lawyer snapped.

"I must have an answer!" the interrogator thundered.
"It is important for me to establish the matter of character!"
He scowled at my lawyers and they scowled back at him.
They remained adamant. "We will have to investigate the
matter further if you refuse to answer." He looked at my
bearded face with obvious suspicion and distaste. "I give
you one more chance."

As we all sat there silently a gleam came to his eye. He
turned to the court reporter and said "I think we may be on
to something." It was pure theatre. But he had the wrong
audience.

I sat there thinking how silly the whole thing was, now
fully aware that his questions had been designed to blacken
my character. We were there because I had filed a libel suit
against the magazine *Saturday Review* when they had neg-
ligently allowed some damaging misinformation to be published about me. They had said that I had been fired in
Roswell for bad judgment. When I had shown up with the
proof of what really had happened — with my lawyers —
they had assigned their own lawyer, and I had some hopes
that I might receive justice. Now their answer seemed to be,
"If we were wrong about there being a skeleton in your closet
then, we'll find another to make you shut up!"

The question about military service was ridiculous —
the lawyer had established that I was the author of the book
Bum Ticker, which dealt with my years as a heart patient
— he hadn't thought that I would have been ineligible for
the draft.

There were a few more questions to answer, but the

sting was gone now as far as I was concerned. I could hardly restrain myself from chortling when he continued to refer back to my draft status. He obviously believed he was on to something — and worse (or better, depending upon how you looked at it) he thought that a conscientious objector had no right to sue to defend his good name. I reflected on the irony of such an attitude emerging from the representative of a respected, liberal publication. I presumed that if they made a mistake which put a man out of his profession for life they would fight to the last to keep the man out of work after their mistake was uncovered. But maybe I did the magazine an injustice. There was just this lawyer who was paid to be nasty, and I was at the receiving end today.

My lawyers assured me as we left the building that we could continue with our suit on the morrow. We might eventually get justice.

But it was not to be. I suppose I will be haunted by the specter of Roswell for the rest of my professional life. The city of Roswell too will turn the details over and over as the years go by — until some day the whole thing may merit a couple of chapters in a book of local history. I would have to trust that the historical researchers would not use *Saturday Review* as one of their sources.

I was not to get justice in this matter — from my viewpoint at least — because shortly after the questioning the U.S. Supreme Court made a ruling in another case. This stated — roughly — that a "public person" cannot sue for libel unless he can prove the malicious intent of the person issuing the libel (such a proof would be nearly impossible to document). I could obviously be recognized as a "public person" because I had been active in civic affairs in the city. Our case could no longer be considered by the courts. The grilling had been for nothing.

But at least I could go back to Dundee and do my job

as librarian there secure in the knowledge that no court testimony or national magazine would ever publish the fact that I once smoked marijuana at a party and got sick (I can't even stand the smell of ordinary cigarettes), or that I had never borne arms to defend democracy because I was 4F.

Back in Dundee I was doing what I could to have the members of the profession come to the defense of a lady librarian in a nearby Chicago suburb who was being victimized by the censors. They were playing dirty. They hadn't liked her policies, but they were trying to get rid of her on the basis of trumped-up charges of sexual misconduct. It was a nasty situation, but it helped me keep my perspective.

Meanwhile the nation itself was showing signs of needing perspective. The FBI had attempted to get hold of the reading records of patrons at various libraries across the nation, claiming that it might find bomb-makers that way. The association had rallied to resist that effort. And a librarian had been jailed for refusing to testify in the Berrigans' case in Harrisburg when the matters involved were professional confidences. The government was adamant in refusing to register owners of guns — but it wanted to have a register of those who used ideas.

I went back to Dundee and told the landlord at our apartment that we were leaving. It was springtime and the fields were drying out. June and I had decided to experiment with living in the woods. I would stay on and work at the library, at least for the time being. Back to the land, disengagement, seemed like a good idea.

28

The Great Outdoors

Our decision to live in the woods may seem strange, especially since I intended to continue to work as a library administrator. We anticipated that people would think it strange, so we did not bandy the information about. The office people at the library had to know roughly where I was — and they had to have a reason for not being able to get hold of me by telephone. They were bemused by the information that we would be living in a tent some distance from civilization — but they understood that my private life should be kept confidential.

There were a number of adjustments to be made. I moved some of my wardrobe to cupboards in the library to guard against the possibility that I might arrive at work some morning looking woodsy and bedraggled. I had to make alternative arrangements for the delivery of our mail. And of course there were all the usual camping arrangements to be made. We had to buy plentiful supplies of fuel for the lamps and the stove, and purchase our insect repellent in wholesale lots.

We had made an agreement with the owner of a tree farm some twenty miles from Dundee. We were to be allowed to develop our own campsite in a clearing which we had discovered while we had been hiking through his property during the previous year. It was understood that there would be no facilities of any kind. The nearest water was half a mile away in a small resort area which had been developed on the other edge of his property. We could use the resort facilities — showers, water, and the swimming hole — but we would be very much thrown on our own resources. That was the way we wanted it.

While we were hauling our stuff into the clearing during the wet month of May (everything had to be hand carried that last half mile) we had two thoughts to console us: the rent was cheap, and the weather would eventually improve enough to allow the ground to dry out so that we might bring our car part way through the woods. We might even find life in the woods a little soft as we were able to haul in luxuries. When we "inherited" a mattress to place on the floor of the tent from one of the residents of the resort we knew that the rot had set in — we were no longer the great pioneers we had imagined ourselves to be.

We soon settled into routines. I got up a little earlier than usual in order to make my breakfast on the kerosene stove. If the weather was bad I would consider eating at a truck stop on the way to work. I had to be early enough to get to the library and shave before starting work — I was a slave to my electric razor (my goatee beard did not liberate me from that chore).

June had her own routines. Camping can involve almost as much work as keeping house. And she had the dog to look after.

There was little or no impact on my work at the library. I was probably better rested and a better guy to work for. When I had a long day — such as when I had to attend a meeting of the library board in the evening — I would leave camp at seven A.M. and sometimes not get back until 11 P.M.

But there were other good days to compensate for that. Sometimes I would be able to get away from the library early in the afternoon and spend some hours cutting brush, chopping firewood, or swimming in the swimming hole. During the week we were guaranteed privacy (the resort area had a dozen or so families at the weekends only). We loved it.

It was while we were at camp that I started thinking of really doing what I wanted to do. I wanted to write more. And I wanted to get away from the Illinois winters. I talked to June about moving to California. We had been in Illinois all of two years. The library was doing well. Should I resign and hope that we could survive in California on my writing and some income from lecturing?

"You mean you'd give up libraries?" June asked me.

"Not entirely," I said. "There just aren't many library jobs around at the moment. And anyway, a library job would keep me from my writing. But I would still keep in touch with libraries. I guess I'll always have libraries in my blood. I'll eventually go back. It is just that I have these other things I want to do — "

"Why don't you wait until you attend the next library conference — talk to people from California while you are there — then make your decision?"

It was a good idea. The conference was only a month away. We wrote to friends and relatives in California to find out how they viewed the move. By the time I was ready to attend the conference in Dallas we had so many enthusiastic answers anticipating our return to California that the decision had almost been made for us.

I traveled to the conference in Texas thinking I would consult some of my librarian friends and resign my Dundee post at the conclusion of the meetings. The conference might not change my resolve — but it was nevertheless likely to offer a few surprises.

The first surprise was in the accomodations. I had registered at the residence halls of Southern Methodist University in order to save our library some of the expense of hotel costs. This turned out to be some distance from the conference site, and quite cut off from most of the usual conference fun and games. I reflected that it would do me good to experience one conference in enforced sobriety.

The other surprises all lay in the programs which our Social Responsibilities Roundtable had prepared. The New York-Philadelphia Axis seemed to be breaking up into factions of women's liberation and gay liberation (and many of our adherents from other parts of the country found themselves drawn in to this split too). This left a great many ordinary heterosexual radicals and liberals with new responsibilities and torn loyalties ("Some of my best friends are queer" was to be heard repeatedly). The programs reflected both the new directions and some indecisiveness.

The Gay Liberation Task Force had arranged to have a "happening" at one of the conference booths. It was billed as "HUG A HOMOSEXUAL." National television was brought in to record the scene for posterity: female librarians kissing female librarians, male librarians kissing male librarians — and a mass of curious onlookers displaying every emotion from extreme repulsion to delighted titillation.

Meantime, back at the booth of the Social Responsibilities Roundtable, there was a mass of pamphlets from every odd cause under the sun (and a militant female defending the untidy pile from the incursions of librarians like myself who thought the information might be more useful if arranged in some manner — to her, disorganization was one of the principles which would save the world from materialistic concerns). And someone who had noted the lack of direction in the presentation had invited the Hare Krishna people to sell their religion to those librarians who lacked a cause. Their yellow robes, strange hairdos, and trays of "blessed" candies certainly made our booth distinctive.

The conference meetings were memorable for a number of things. There was an appeal by Zoia Horn, the librarian who had refused to testify in the trial of the Berrigan brothers, for support by the association. The members voted that support. There were moves to make the council of the association a more representative body. And there was my denunciation of the Action Council of the Social Responsibilities Round Table for allowing their facilities to be used to promote a fundamentalist religious organization (or any religious organization), the Krishna people; the half-hearted defense of the decision to allow the Hare Krishna group the use of our booth included the statement, "Well, they looked freaky — I thought they'd be good for our image!"

There was no doubt that the association was changing — that the profession was changing — and that I was changing. I was quite glad to get back to my little room in the university residence hall each evening and think over what had happened. The radical rhetoric was fading. I had met one of the people responsible for the Yippie affair in Chicago and had asked him why he chose my meeting to disrupt. His answer was, "We anarchists don't need to have reasons."

I asked him, "Did it ever strike you that there might be an anarchist or two behind the program you loused up?" He just gave me a sour look.

The cocktail parties were still being given by library commercial suppliers. I attended a few of these. But the largest congregation of librarians appeared instead at the employment area. There were hundreds there at every hour the place was open. It certainly signified a change in the profession's image — just a couple of years previously the librarian could almost choose a job anywhere (as long as he had not been involved in a censorship controversy). My decision to leave Dundee was not compromised, however. I could pat myself on the back for making one more job available to these desperate unemployed librarians.

Censorship was still being discussed — and many more instances were being reported — but the association was finally taking some action, and there was less need for concern for the welfare of the embattled librarians. The Task Force on Intellectual Freedom disbanded (I was a member) and tried to reorganize itself into new groups to encourage libraries to collect materials which had previously been avoided because of the efforts of the censors.

The new task forces which were proposed would concern themselves with underground publications, religious and atheist publications, and sexually related media. It was predictable that I would be named coordinator of the Task Force on Sex Related Media. It was a job that could only be done by someone who didn't have a library position, some people reasoned. It gave me one more incentive to resign my position in Dundee. After all, I wouldn't want to embarrass my employers!

I wrote my resignation on the way to the airport. I would regret leaving all my loyal employees and a lot of my friends — and I said so in the letter — but I had other, personal things to do. I gave sixty days notice. It would be the end of summer when I would be free to leave. I would miss the Illinois woods too. But there was lots of outdoors in California.

As I was boarding the plane to leave Dallas for Chicago I heard a Texan using an expression I had grown used to hearing in Roswell, New Mexico. "You all come back, y'hear!" There had been lots of outdoors there too.

29

Drowning A Little

Back in California I was soon involved in another cause. I wanted to make sure that information was freely available to all — and libraries weren't doing it — so I joined Community Switchboard in Santa Cruz.

I volunteered to answer a telephone four hours a week. There were more than sixty other volunteers who had obligated themselves for one or more shifts. The switchboard stayed open twenty-four hours a day, and would try to answer anything. The library closed at nine o'clock, and would answer only what could be found printed in a book.

On one of my early shifts I had a female companion answering the telephone. "Can you tell me where to get in touch with a good whorehouse in town?" a male caller asked her.

"Sure, honey!" she answered in her sexiest voice. I never got a chance to find out the answer to that question, however, for the caller either hadn't been serious or had become scared. *Click.* He hung up. I became busy on some calls of my own, and never found out what her sources might have been. I mention it because her, "Sure, honey!" was typical of the attitude of the switchboard volunteer. They would try anything to help anyone in need.

Our switchboard had files — kept as up to date as an immediate telephone call could accomplish — of everything from legal and medical referrals to lost dogs, houses for rent, and jobs available. There wasn't anything that they wouldn't try to answer — or at least find someone who could answer. And we offered help to those in emotional distress too. The volunteers were capable in many of the less severe crisis calls, and had lists of suicide-prevention counselors, clergymen and psychiatric social workers. It was the idealist librarian's dream of effective public service.

I learned that the library serving the county had answered a little more than thirty thousand reference questions during the previous year — and found that the switchboard had come just a little short of that with a budget which was less than one hundredth that of the library's.

I became a fanatic in the cause of switchboards.

Switchboards were springing up all across the nation — while libraries were going down the drain. Library budgets were being reduced and librarians were out of work everywhere.

I took the time to write an article about the matter — I said that all the Switchboards needed was a Carnegie to provide them with the physical facilities, and tax reform to give them the tax base that libraries presently enjoyed. I had studied the professional literature and found that my impression of volunteer workers was confirmed by the studies — the professional worker was not necessarily any better than the dedicated volunteer. I emphasized my conviction that the proper social reforms and information services should spring from the bosom of the community and not from the paternalistic benificence of the professional classes. My radical rhetoric had found a new lease on life. I threatened the public library with certain doom unless it reformed.

I had been published by the national professional journals a number of times before, but this time I was not going to be rushed into print. I could hardly blame them. They had enjoyed a little sensationalism when I had published articles on how librarians were quite as likely to censor things as the censors themselves, or how a head librarian ought to give himself time off for a private existence separate from his library duties — but this? They weren't ready for it. I wasn't in libraries any more.

I was busy with the switchboard and my other writings anyway. If I was right, time would tell. I put the article away.

There was plenty to be done at the switchboard. The local cable television station offered us a fifteen minute "information" spot on their newscast. I got the job because I had television experience. I sat in front of the cameras and swapped banter with the newscaster. Everybody voted it a great show — and we got more calls at the switchboard.

One of our services was a place to "crash" for people passing through town who had nowhere to stay. One of the switchboard coordinators had the idea of opening a youth hostel. As a former "housefather" of a youth hostel in Scotland I was soon acting as consultant, and eventually as one of the directors of the board; the project was funded by the County Supervisors, and proved quite successful.

Then there was the foster-parent problem to keep me going. One of the calls to the switchboard involved a sixteen-year-old girl who had been held at the county juvenile hall for no other reason than that she had no parents to go to. She had been there a number of weeks when she was permitted the outside call which sent me to her aid. I was horrified to discover that the girl was being treated exactly as the delinquent young people with whom she was incarcerated. She was not allowed to contact friends outside, her mail was censored, and even her schooling was being limited because of the security demands of the facility. It was the schooling which caused her the greatest concern — she had been an "A" student until she had found herself without foster parents.

We discovered that she was without foster parents through no fault of her own — the people who had looked after her had been overwhelmed by their own personal problems. We discovered that there was a shortage of foster parents in the county. Children could expect to be committed to juvenile hall as long as the shortage persisted. Switchboard had another project — to promote the foster parent program — and I had a young lady to save from the jaws of the institutional dragon.

It took us a number of weeks — they must have seemed an eternity to the girl — to get the issue well enough known so that foster homes became available. There were letters to the newspaper, and recriminations from members of the probation department who felt they were doing all they could. But our Kathy found a home. Switchboard had won again.

There were other projects. The switchboard needed money, so we helped sponsor a concert of classical guitar music and did most of the work in the auditorium ourselves. That brought in a little. We sponsored a booth at an arts and crafts fair, obtaining the concession from the natural foods bakery. A number of us spent the weekend wrapping and selling the food. It was wearying work, but it brought in some more money and paid our telephone bills.

The switchboard could *always* use more money and volunteer labor (there were so many uncompleted projects which needed both). Switchboard volunteers bothered the city fathers and the civic organizations incessantly asking for support for the multitude of programs.

I came up with the bright idea of asking the library if it would cooperate with us. No one had ever considered that it might even be appropriate to ask. I thought it could maybe give us office space, donate some equipment or work with us to expand the community information files. I almost convinced the other volunteers that it made sense.

"After all," I said, "the library should be providing many of the information services we offer. They get tax funds to do that."

"They'll never work with long-hairs, man!" somebody said. "We could ask them to help us stop the world from coming to an end, and they'd tell us to get some shoes on and show our library card before they'd even talk to us!"

I reminded the speaker that not all switchboard volunteers were long-hairs — one of them was a sixty-four-year-old lady — and not all of our services were youth oriented.

"I know that, man," he said, "but even if we got every senior citizen we'd helped to picket in front of the library, they'd still say they were being threatened by a bunch of hippies."

I got the permission of the volunteers to approach the library on the switchboard's behalf anyway ("It can't do any harm to ask," I'd said). I suppose the result was predictable. The library served the retired population and the children of well-to-do parents who only used it for class assignments. I should have known what to expect when I saw that the library had signs on the doors requiring the wearing of shoes even though it was in a beach town.

I wrote to the library, and had an interview in the librarians office. The result of the interview was no different from the preliminary written opinion I had received when I wrote the letter. The librarian could see "no logic" in cooperation between the switchboard and the library. I had suggested that there might be state or federal funds available for an innovative program predicated on community service. I was willing to work on that angle, and we had consultants at the university — even the state library might help. The answer was *no*.

I always had my cabin, my writing and my redwood

trees for solace, however, I had received some requests to give lectures. I felt that what I was doing was worthwhile. I could only feel sorry for all the young librarians who were desperately trying to find a job — any job — in a business which was so blindly self-satisfied and resistant to change. At the conferences it had seemed that there might be change in the making, but I had to wonder how much of that had been talk. There was one thing certain — the new librarians who managed to get a job would be in no position to rock any boats. There were too many people ready to fill their jobs. Maybe they should join switchboards instead . . . .

"You are no longer a librarian?" somebody asked me.

"Sure, I'm a librarian," I replied. "I'm like one of these new working priests, taking the religion to the people. The churches and the libraries have lost their relevance. We have to get back to the principles. My creed is free access to information. It is the only way to have democracy and honesty."

"Very commendable — but does it pay?"

"Well," I said, "the library schools came up with a nice liberal idea not long ago. They would send librarians in to the communities and lay library service on the people. They called these *floating* librarians. It was a well-intentioned idea, but it has the basic flaw of elitism — it doesn't give the communities any chance to lay *their* needs on the libraries."

My questioner looked at me quizzically.

"I have come up with my own concept of the floating librarian," I said. "It means keeping your head above the water."

30

Sex Again

My professional connection with the association hadn't ended. I was still coordinator of that Task Force on Sex Related Media. When we organized it somebody asked why the profession needed such a group. "Because libraries pretend they can't stock stuff because there's no *reputable* information," I answered. "They do that with political stuff, religious stuff, sexy stuff, even new community information. If they can't find a review — even if it is the most needed, relevant information there is — they will say they can't put it in the library until its worth is recognized. We plan to show them that sexy materials are an important *and reputable* part of life."

"But why are you just doing sexy stuff?"

"Because we can't do it all — we need others to push the other stuff. I happen to like the sexy stuff."

As coordinator I had to keep the lines of communication open and advise members about overall needs. We started out with a number of goals. We would try to develop a list of essential books, films and recordings — and anything else that might be useful (someone suggested prostheses) — to aid library buyers. We would also hope to promote reviews of the new material (someone called it "raw" material) so that buyers, whether librarians or members of the public, would know what they were buying. Some of us even thought of publishing our own reviewing journal (we eagerly anticipated the free review copies we would receive). We also hoped to find communities which would welcome our efforts.

We wanted to establish support and clearinghouse sections. We would communicate with all the various groups involved in the media. They were not difficult to identify: the sex education people, the schools, the publishers, the sexual minority groups (homosexuals, nudists, transvestites, etc.), the social scientists, the artists and so on. We would do all we could to acquaint them with what the libraries could (and should) do for them, and then communicate their needs to our reluctant colleagues.

Last but not least, we would investigate the possibility of making sex-related materials more available to people. We would try to do something about the cataloging procedures which give misleading subject headings to materials dealing with sexy subjects — they make it too easy for librarians to "lose" something about which they have uncertainties. We would see to it that sexy materials would be available on inter-library loan if a library failed to provide its own copies (we even envisioned establishing a central collection of such materials so that people could get used to having it available — it would be dismantled after libraries started collecting their own sexy stuff). And we proposed the establishment of "sexual adventure collections" in every local library.

This last proposal was the one which caused the greatest expression of interest. My idea was that those libraries which presently segregate their collections of light reading into "mysteries," "westerns," "science fiction," "romances" and the like had no reason to exclude sexy light reading from their array. A look into the bookshops quickly confirms that

sexual adventure is more in demand than any of the other
categories. Whole bookshops are dedicated to the subject.
Why not a few shelves in the library? Why discriminate
against readers of such material? Aren't they paying taxes
for the purchase of the other guy's mysteries and Westerns?
Don't librarians boast that they believe in every person's right
to necessary information? Why *not* a sexual adventure
collection?

We soon found that interest in what we might do was
much higher than interest in our theories. But we had more
theories than volunteers. Our work force was lacking. It could
be believed that librarians were holding back because of fear
of unemployment or social pressures. Was there voyeurism
in their I'm-interested-but-don't-ask-me-to-do-anything attitude? Did impotent librarians get their kicks from imagining
what it'd be like to have a free collection?

In order to keep going we had to reason that the novelty
of our ideas was too much for our colleagues — they were
interested, but not yet ready to move. We would have to
educate them. I fantasized that some day it would be possible
for a bunch of people to ask for the use of the library auditorium to demonstrate sexual positions. The librarians would
be so freed from taboos that they would respond: "Sure, it
is a very worthwhile public program. But don't do it on our
carpeting — you'll get a bad nylon burn on your knees."
But the task force had a long way to go before libraries
would be able to respond to such requests with anything
short of hysteria. And the day would probably never arrive
when a librarian would be available with the expertise about
the likelihood of friction on nylon carpeting.

In order to educate people — and librarians in particular
— the task force decided to hold programs featuring people
who had suffered from the lack of information caused by
censorship. We soon had a large list of possible speakers:

sexual freedom militants, transsexuals, nudists, members of a child-sexuality society, people from the homosexual community, urban swingers and wife-swappers, transvestites, and even some individuals who had gone to jail for victimless sex offenses. I felt part of their suffering could be blamed on the libraries' part in the conspiracy of silence.

We would need to open the libraries up to sex, to religion and its counterpart, atheism, to unpopular political causes — and even to tabu words. If we could do that we could add stature to society by helping integrate these elements — and people — we have so long rejected. But it would take more than our little task force to do it. The American Library Association didn't seem to be encouraging the formation of additional groups such as ours.

Meantime, our task force would have to teach librarians how to answer questions about abortion, prostate trouble, masturbation, whorehouses and other kinds of bleepable information without embarrassment. Could librarians do it? It would hardly leave them time for a sex life of their own. But did librarians have a sex life? That was one of the missing pieces of information in any library. Maybe we needed to run a survey on that?

31

Changes

There is only so much you can do to improve the nation's libraries if you insist on living in the mountains and eating when you get hungry.

Sometimes such a life doesn't even agree with a wife, your nearest and dearest. She may be a good sport and rough it in a tent for a season, but living permanently in a cabin in the hills may have drawbacks in her eyes. Eventually all of her pent-up frustrations will explode and she will insist on going to movies, theatres and social gatherings every night. How is a man dedicated to freedom of access to the media to oppose such a plea? If you plead poverty she may cite the notorious Joneses whom you were so happy to say goodby to. You think that it would be nice if some fellow named Jones would start being competitive about the simple life.

You tell her that she should be glad about the nice cabin among the trees — and she says she wants to be nearer the laundrymat, and she worries about forest fires. You mention the healthy mountain air — and she complains about the fog and the steep, twisting roads. You mention the peace and quiet, and she says that sometimes the solitude gets to her.

You go on to mention all the writing you've been able to do — and she reminds you of how slow some of the publishers have been in paying. She rubs it in by asking what good will it all have been if it is never read. "What if the libraries censor it after it is published?" she asks.

"They can't do that!" you say.

"They can — "

"It's not allowed!" But you know in your heart of hearts that they can.

Then you think a bright thought. "Sometimes banned books really sell big — I'll make a lot of money!"

"Not if libraries censor a book — you know they can do it so quietly no one would ever know or care — people *expect* libraries to censor books. It is part of the tradition."

You nod glumly.

"Where did I go wrong?" you say.

"I'm going to a movie," she says.

"I can't afford it," you say. "But what's playing?"

"It's the best of the New York Porno Festival," says she.

"Enjoy it," you say, even though you are dying to say "But a woman can't go into one of these places alone." It is the era of women's liberation. You just have to hope that she comes out of the place alone — but even that is a selfish, chauvinist thought, and you tell yourself you ought to be ashamed.

You have no interest in going to the show yourself (a) because New York's measure of what is best is unlikely to be yours, and (b) your appetite for such things is jaded.

She goes off to the movies and you count the change in your pocket and wonder if the switchboard work and the work for the association (neither of which pays you a dime) has been worthwhile. You tell yourself that there's only so much a guy can do if he has to type everything himself and depend on rural mail services.

You sit down at the typewriter and some constipated words smudge the page. You tear the page out of the machine and flush it down the toilet, wondering if the paper is bio-degradable and won't hurt the septic tank.

She comes back from the movie at a respectable hour and you congratulate yourself that you still don't need to have a check up at the V.D. clinic. You are ashamed of your uncharitable thoughts again.

She says, "You really should see the new movies they are making. The medium is changing."

You wonder if it is true. Have you really been out in the woods that long — and has the lack of money cut you off from culture? You reflect that the free Wednesday after-noon films at the library are on such things as dental hygiene and the glaciation patterns of Norwegian fiords. There's something wrong.

"Maybe they will ban my book," you say.

"Huh?"

"Maybe they'll ban it — " you point to the manuscript " — there's some sex in it."

She shakes her head. "No chance," she says.

"But it is also about *libraries!*"

"I know," she says, "but nobody will ever believe there's such a thing as a sexy librarian. I'm tired. Let's go to bed."

You are tired too, but the mountain air and peace and quiet are responsible for appetites you never had in the city. You remember that she just came back from a porno show. As you climb into bed you ask "Sexy?"

She turns her back on you and says "Ugh-ugh."

You curse the steep and twisty mountain roads that are responsible for her tenseness.

Being blessed with a writer's constitution you are awake at an ungodly hour and you stumble about in the early morning hours getting yourself breakfast. You can't get to the typewriter until she gets up anyway. You have to warm up the cabin to accomplish that.

When she gets up and you serve her breakfast (it's easier that way) she asks, "Gonna do any writing today?"

You nod noncommitally. "Been thinking about libraries again."

"But I thought you had nearly finished that book — weren't you going to write science fiction or something?"

You nod. "Science fiction pornography." You stare at the dirty dishes. "But I keep thinking I should do something about libraries. They really need somebody like me."

"You mean they need an anti-fascist, anti-bureaucratic pseudo-anarchist egotist-humorist? Gonna be our savior again? How many times do you have to be martyred?"

"I have to do my bit for peace and free expression and human rights," you say defensively, " — and earn a buck!"

She snorts in answer.

"You said things were changing. Maybe they need me out there!"

"What's that got to do with libraries? Who said they were changing?"

"If they don't change they'll just go *pthth* —" you say, making a rude noise with extended tongue.

"How are you going to save the world this time?"

"I'm going to set up a lending-library-by-mail and offer adult books on a subscription basis. People would become members. Libraries could borrow from us on interlibrary loan — they'd have no excuse for not offering adult materials then. It's an idea which must come — someone must do it eventually. The government should fund it. It would make the library business true to its ideals!"

"And where will you get the money to start?"

"Gonna apply for a job in a library."

"You're kidding!"

You figure that is what they'll say too when they get your application. You tell yourself you'd have to learn to eat at regular hours. If you could take it, the libraries could! Who was prejudiced against whom — you against libraries or they against you? You could always come back to the mountains if it didn't work out, you tell yourself.

"I've been thinking of a way to bring in more money too," she says.

"What's that?"

"I could dance in a nightclub — I could develop an act."

You remember that she had training as a dancer when she was younger — and there are friends in a few of the more exotic clubs. "Yours would be a unique act for these places — if I'm thinking of the same places you are. I suppose you are kidding?"

She shakes her head. "I've got some nice costumes — I could put rhinestones on some — "

"You'd be a *stripper?* You are too nice for that."

"An *exotic* dancer," she says. "My act would be wholesome, full of art. You don't think I could do it, make a go of it?"

"I didn't say that — it just takes a little bit of getting used to, the idea."

"Having a sexy woman in the home is just like having a sexy book in the library, huh?" she says, snuggling up. "I'll bet you'll love the idea when it grows on you."

"Any objections to me trying libraries again?"

"None."

"There will be one advantage to me getting a job in a library, anyway."

"You are not going to tell me it pays worth anything!"

"No," you say with a smile, "it will simply guarantee that there'll be one library in the country which carries my book!"